Why is there a gorilla on the cover?
All primates are our close relatives.
For centuries, we humans have built layers
on top of our shared world about which they
know nothing—the intangible realm. That is
what really separates us.

YOUR BUSINESS STRATEGY FOR THE INTANGIBLE FUTURE
BY MIIKKA LEINONEN

Published by Immaterial Inc.
Copyright © Miikka Leinonen, 2024
All Rights Reserved
Editing by Richard Martin
Illustrations: Sic (Shitty Illustrator's club)
ChatGPT 4.0 was used while researching the text
Midjourney was used to create visuals

ISBN 978-952-65387-0-9

Table of

How to read this book

Welcome! This isn't your typical business book. Instead, it's a window into the sweeping changes humanity is poised to experience.

Think of the book as a thought experiment, a playground for ideas. It's designed to be as unconventional as the transformations we will discuss. From occasional moments of humor to unique design choices, every element is crafted to challenge and entertain.

As you read, I invite you to keep an open mind. The concepts you will encounter aren't necessarily new, but they're repackaged to provide fresh insights. I encourage you to actively engage with them, always questioning, testing the tools provided, and reflecting on your own experiences.

A word of warning: If you're seeking a book grounded in fact-based argument and real-world evidence, look elsewhere. But if you're ready for something more speculative and imaginative, then you're in the right place.

In this age of AI, the traditional book is both dying and being reborn. This publication playfully contributes to that evolution. I hope you'll enjoy the journey ahead and the surprises along the way.

Let's dive in!

Contents

Contributors:
Martin Wezowski
Thomas Schindler
David Erhard
Urs Merkel
Alberto-Giovanni Busetto

And Tobias Burkhardt
as the inner voice:

● "All European white males.
Well done, Miikka."

Your future is intangible

BY MARTIN WEZOWSKI

AS a strategic futurist, the one thing I have learned above all others is the organizational importance of long-term foresight. A company that continues to be driven by its own history carries a terminal risk. When you run out of possible futures, you are doomed. In business, having a future is the most valuable thing.

If you do not define yourself by your future, others will define you by your past, and hand you a future they prefer. To combat these external pressures, you must make your dreams and ambitions as easy to grasp and experience as your past.

The better future thinker you are, the more space and time you can carve out to put all your assets to work. In this sense, foresight is an efficiency game.

As your future does not exist yet, it is intangible by nature. It is renewable and imaginable, as well as your most valuable immaterial business asset.

CREATIVITY IS THE DRIVER

Human creativity is the most important business driver of the future. I hope the ideas, practices, and examples presented in this book will enable you to appreciate, discover, and foster that creativity, helping you enjoy future success.

By having the ability to translate ideas into tangible environments and tools, we build our futures. What is intangible now is a resource for the tangible, for production, business, society, and all of humanity.

OUR FUTURE DEPENDS ON HOPE AND OPTIMISM

It is easier to see problems than solutions. Problems are tangible, like forest fires, supply chain shortages, and lack of parking spaces. We have insanely complex problems ahead of us that through interaction and acceleration present a potentially destructive force.

But, without wishing to diminish the scale and importance of the problems we face, we cannot become distracted by the pessimists. We have a job to do. Every problem presents an opportunity. We have the capacity to grasp them. That is the position of the optimist.

IF YOU DO NOT DEFINE YOURSELF BY YOUR FUTURE, OTHERS WILL DEFINE YOU BY YOUR PAST, AND HAND YOU A FUTURE THEY PREFER.

The world we enjoy today was shaped by the optimists of the past. Optimism is a productive force that we must use to shape the future. Optimism is our tool to make hopes visible and tangible in the products and services we offer.

Climate change, global inequality, and power centralization in the technology sector are all very real problems, but the solutions remain much more intangible than the problems. All solutions are fragile and vague to start with. They rely on fresh ideas, persistence, diplomacy, and new connections.

Those who lead with optimism, passion, creativity, and skin in the game will write the history of the future. This book prompts us to take the first steps, engaging and experimenting with new ideas and practices, questioning and challenging the business and society we know today.

●

Strong ideas don't need wingmen. The author of this book wishes to adorn himself with borrowed plumes, luring people into believing this nonsense. You should have seen that coming, Mr. Wezowski!

WE BELIEVE IN INTANGIBLES

Pre-historic humans imagined powers greater than us to account for the unknown. We went on to develop elaborate narratives centered on myth, magic, religion, and monarchy to make these powers more tangible. Today, corporations nurture our shared belief in the intangible known as money. Like the religious bodies and monarchies of old, businesses and financial institutions wield enormous resources and are not afraid to protect their place, establishing and controlling the tangible–intangible transactions that govern our world.

We have agreed that a piece of metal or paper or a number in a digital wallet has real tangible value. We can exchange it for concrete things like food and clothing. This is an insane human achievement, made-up-imaginary value that can be traded to physical goods and labor.

NEW POWERS EMERGING

But a new power is rising to complement the incumbent rulers and gatekeeper. Us, the people.

Individual expression is the intangible inner world of ideas, intentions, and plans. Individuals are now joining forces with the established financial networks, emerging as sovereign, networked, and productive agents in the global economy. We must trust the ingenuity of our fellow humans, adapting our business networks, and providing the time and space for this intangible asset to flourish.

THOSE WHO LEAD WITH OPTIMISM, PASSION, CREATIVITY, AND SKIN IN THE GAME WILL WRITE THE HISTORY OF THE FUTURE.

Can you imagine the innovative and creative powers of ten billion amplified individuals in vibrant creative flows? Rather than competing, we would be able to complete and complement one another, building solutions, and making desirable futures possible.

By increasing the power of individuals in our business networks, we could gain authority, authorship, and participation, and not only speculation in our economies, ecologies, and societies.

Learning about the intangible powers that we hold is a key insight for leaders in corporations and finance institutions. It is the first step to building a future that we all want to live in.

Supportive tools, software, and organizational "operating systems" are crucial. However, during an era when human ingenuity and creativity are being challenged by generative artificial intelligence, we may need to redefine our understanding of productivity. We must trust that our workforce's creative optimism is the true source of productivity, while technology is nothing more than a tool enabling its achievement.

Our ideas about the future, about the progress toward its attainment, need to be transparent, maneuverable, mapped, and understood. We need to see, feel, and almost touch what the future will be. It is this that will support our businesses, sustain our communities, and build a sense of belonging.

Can you spot how many abstract intangible terms I used in this text? Words like business, asset, innovation, market, relationship, practice... The intangible plays a significant role in our future.

This book will be your guide to new business thinking during an era when artificial and human intelligences come closer together. By business thinking, I don't only mean staples like operations, decision making, strategy, and brand perception. I mean thinking. Philosophical thinking. At the board level, in the C-suite, and across the business.

LET'S LEAD FROM THAT FUTURE!

Product portfolio, design, engineering, and pricing can be deeply connected to your purpose, culture, and business vision, impacting one of the great intangibles: how people perceive you.

We need to add more understanding of the intangible in complex planning, vision crafting, foresight, creativity, disambiguation, social coherence, culture and community building, long lasting innovation, bias-management, ethics, purpose seeking, and curiosity, just to mention a few of the most cherished business values we are familiar with. If we have the means, tools, and courage to unlock the intangible values in the real world we can achieve even more.

If the future were a product, this book might provide an interface for interacting with and experiencing it. Learn how to use it! Read, reflect, absorb, experiment with the methods, play with the questions and provocations. Look at it as a playground in which you develop your new leadership practices and learn to embrace the intangible. It's that easy to use.

Quiet Change

Not long ago, things like paper phone books, maps, and calendars were everywhere. But they gradually disappeared from our tables and walls. These common items were quietly transformed, no longer physical and tangible but available on phones and computer screens.

Our calendars and maps are no longer just in one place at home. They're with us in digital form wherever we go. Now, we can use them in new ways, anytime and anywhere, and in more ways than were possible with their paper versions.

A map on a phone can update itself and anticipate our journey ahead. A digital calendar can remind us of an appointment and talk with our map. They have become active parts of our lives, not just things we look at.

Even though they've changed how they look, these items still fulfill their primary functions. A digital map still shows us the way, while a digital photo still brings back memories. What matters about them hasn't changed, it's just that they're available in a different form.

This shift from paper to digital shows how we adapt. Everyday items may now be on screens, but they're still a big part of our lives. They illustrate how our world is always changing and how we keep finding new ways to live with technology.

Nice story, but this book is not about the disappearance of everyday objects.

REAL WORK TEST

1 Think of your previous day at work.

2 List all things you did.

3 Mark with a big letter **P** the activities that produced* something physical**.

Morning	P	Afternoon	P
ACTIVITY		ACTIVITY	

Everything without a P was more or less intangible.

*) Produced = something that you did there and then.
Making a plan for something concrete
that will be done later or by somebody else does not count.

**) Physical = something you can touch.
Attending a meeting does not count.

Your work is probably mostly intangible, but we do not address that with intellectual honesty. If we were to acknowledge the intangible nature of our work, it could help us break free of old constraints, creating new spaces and opportunities for thinking and creativity.

Nice exercise, but this book is not about the disappearance of physical aspects of work.

THE IDEA IN BRIEF

In the intricate game of business, there are two consistent threads woven through its fabric: the tangible and the intangible. The tangible includes physical assets, products, and infrastructure, which are immediately recognizable and quantifiable. By contrast, the intangible encompasses emotions, creativity, knowledge, brand, company culture, intellectual property, data, and artificial intelligence (AI). They remain behind the scenes, yet profoundly influence outcomes. As the business landscape evolves, mastering the distinctive roles and synergies of the tangible and intangible becomes crucial for business owners, leaders, and executives.

The rapid advance of digitalization provides new connections between the tangible and intangible, blurring traditional boundaries and amplifying the strengths of the intangible domain. This invisible layer, expanding above our physical world, brings significant implications for business strategies. While the physical realm remains vital, the burgeoning intangible space opens up an array of strategic possibilities. Embracing the qualities of the intangible world is key for businesses seeking to excel in this immaterial realm. Tomorrow's successful industry leaders will be adept at perceiving and leveraging the symbiosis between material and immaterial worlds.

However, navigating the complex interplay of the tangible and intangible poses unique challenges. A shared language, understood across the organizational spectrum, is essential. Without this common lexicon, the nuances and subtleties of the intangible world remain elusive, increasing the challenge of coherent strategy formulation and execution.

This book offers a theoretical framework and practical tools for executives to decode, comprehend, and navigate this expansive and rapidly changing territory. By bridging the gap between tangible assets and intangible forces, leaders can unlock opportunities for innovation, growth, and lasting success in today's business landscape.

The future of business will be defined by the effective integration of the tangible and intangible. Those capable of this integration will lead the way in shaping the business world of tomorrow. (Yeah, baby, hyperbole!)

How very ChatGPT 1.0!

Why did I write this book?

TO SAVE THE PLANET

We have been overusing Earth's finite resources for a long time. The intangible entity known as the limited liability company (LLC) was created to harness all tangible assets as resources for its business, but it has been too successful for its own good. Capitalism and market economy have to find a new playground. The physical world cannot endure anymore. I want to help companies shift their focus to the immaterial world. Unlike their material sister, they are abundant and can house as many businesses as we can imagine.

FOR MY CHILDREN

To Lili and Eeva. All the weird stuff I tried to explain to you. It is all here. Look, I did my part. Not sure if I saved the world, but I did my part.

TO FINISH A PROJECT

Numerous nights in bed before sleep I have drawn images, canvases, maps, and tools in my head. Hundreds of versions. This is a sequel to my book Melt, which was published when my ideas were incomplete. I had to continue pursuing my white whale. Hope I don't have to write this a third time. But I probably will.

WHO IS THIS BOOK FOR?

Strategy Consultants

Serious business leaders

Enthusiasts who want to bask in the warmth of something novel

You know who
you are. Own it!

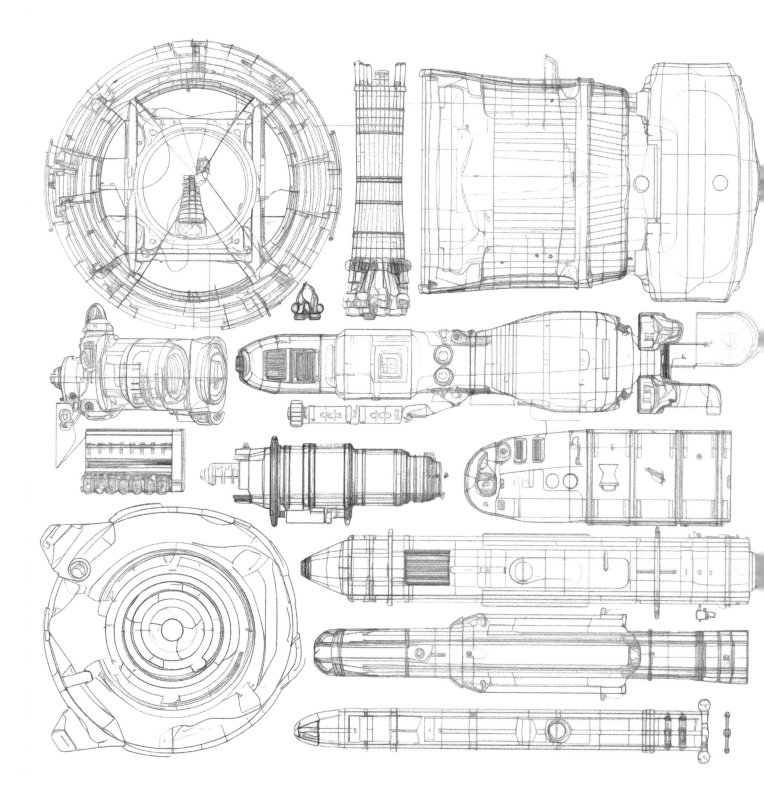

{ Terminology }

This is not a simple topic and the terminology I have chosen to use is not typical business jargon. The book is littered with abstract terms.

Wait, no it's not! There are just two terms we are working with here. Tangible and intangible, which I use interchangeably with material and immaterial. Same stuff, different labels.

So four terms, not more. Everything else in this book is self-explanatory.

But what do these terms mean?

$\{$ Tangible $\}$ = Material

🔊 /ˈtandʒɪbl/

This is kind of obvious. Tangible refers to something that is perceptible by touch. Tangible objects are those that have a physical presence and can be observed with the senses. Key characteristics of tangible objects include:

1 **OCCUPANCY OF SPACE:** Tangible objects occupy physical space, which means they cannot occupy the same space as other tangible objects simultaneously.

2 **PHYSICAL PROPERTIES:** Tangible objects are made of matter and possess substance. They typically have physical properties such as texture, color, shape, and density that can be examined and described.

3 **PERCEPTIBILITY:** Tangible objects are observable and can be perceived through sensory experiences. They can be seen, touched, smelled, heard, or tasted.

4 **MEASURABILITY:** Tangible objects often can be quantified, measured, or weighed because they have physical attributes. For example, you can measure the length, weight, or volume of a tangible object.

From a business perspective, they have one defining characteristic:

X **SCARCITY.** Tangible objects inhabit a finite space and are limited in number. This concept of scarcity is essential for businesses. It shapes how resources are allocated and how prices are determined.

Okay. Now that we have a shared understanding of what tangible means, here comes the hard part.

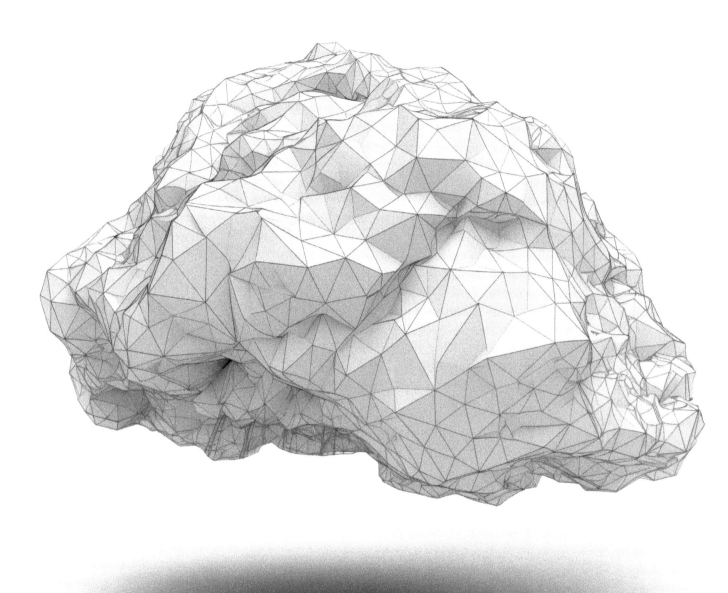

{Intangible} = immaterial

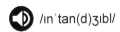 /ɪnˈtan(d)ʒɪbl/

Let's not do this! Defining the *intangible* only leads us to philosophical back alleys and dead ends. During numerous conversations on the topic, I have found myself caught up in convoluted debates. "What is truly intangible," I am asked. "Are there any elements that qualify as fully immaterial?

"Is sound immaterial? What about wind? Are emotions immaterial elements or chemical reactions? What about a written contract? Is that immaterial?"●

That might be an interesting topic for first-year philosophy students to explore but this is supposed to be a business book. Four our purposes, further discussion is fruitless. Anything that is fully intangible elements is of no use to business.

In fact, most things that initially seem intangible do have a home in the physical world. Let's take information and data, for example. In theory, they can be considered intangible. But they become tangible when stored in a physical location, even though their inherent nature remains intangible.

To simplify our understanding in a business context, it's practical to consider that all immaterial elements possess some degree of materiality. Some just happen to be more immaterial than others.

●
In my mind, the speaker has an annoyingly nasal voice.

It is good to focus on elements that are definitely not material, that we can safely say are not fully tangible. Here are examples, but I'm sure you can come up with more.

INTANGIBLE ELEMENTS

PERSONAL STUFF:

Love, emotions, thoughts, aspirations, memories, identity, creativity, moral compass, beliefs, values, ideals, attitudes, perceptions of beauty, charisma, wisdom, Sisu, sense of justice, loyalty, faith, spiritual conviction, consciousness, intuition, hope, sense of humor...

ABSTRACT CONCEPTS:

Ideas, knowledge, time, freedom, luck, theoretical constructs...

SOCIAL CONSTRUCTS:

Imaginaries, social norms, hierarchy, friendship, trust, morality, laws, customs, cultural practices, democracy, nation states, religious doctrines, political ideologies, legacy, gratitude, commitment, social status, ethics, human rights, taboos...

There are many ways to categorize immaterial elements. But this is as scientific as we are going to get in this book.

BUSINESS ASSETS:

Companies, contracts, patents, trademarks, copyrights, reputation, teito, brand, business models, organizational culture...

"THE NEW KIDS ON THE BLOCK"

DIGITAL ELEMENTS:

Digital data, software, cyber security, social media, digital identity, digital twins, metaverse, blockchain, decentralized autonomous organization (DAO), online clout...

AUTOMATION:

Algorithms, AI, autonomous systems...

THE NEXT NEW THING...

CHEAT SHEET

Assess how intangible something is

	Yes	No
Is it impossible to see, touch, or taste it?	☐	☐
Is its exact location difficult to pinpoint?	☐	☐
Is it difficult to control or own?	☐	☐
Does it keep changing all the time?	☐	☐
Is it difficult to quantify or measure?	☐	☐

The more ticks you have here, the more intangible it is.

CHEAT SHEET FOR THE CHEAT SHEET

When we move further away from the tangible, certain characteristics become evident:

- Has very little mass (kind of obvious)
- Difficult to pinpoint its exact location
- Can transform and move quickly
- Can easily combine with other elements
- Not a finite resource; can become abundant
- Difficult to control or own
- Hard to measure precisely

Examples of tangible elements:
Stone, Titanic (the ship, not the movie), coffee cup, building, dog, puppy, very small puppy, bed, car, rollercoaster, battery, flower, your mama, tree, Reader's Digest, bridge, hummus, factory, ninja outfit, sushi, football, tennis ball, basketball, rugby ball, volleyball, golf ball...

Location, location, location

Flow, flow, flow

Life is an interplay of the tangible and intangible ▸

There is a profound and often underappreciated dynamic between the tangible and intangible aspects of life. This delicate balance forms a continuous bond, where the physical and metaphysical realms intertwine and influence each other. This linkage is more than just a philosophical concept; it is an integral part of our everyday reality.

Our life's journey is deeply rooted in the physical world, a realm governed by our senses—touch, sight, sound, smell, and taste. However, it is the intangible facets of our existence—our emotions, thoughts, dreams, and memories—that lend richness and depth to our lives. These intangible elements are as influential in shaping our interpersonal relationships, societal norms, personal achievements, and self-identity as the physical world.

Consider how our inherently intangible emotions can manifest physically. A blush of embarrassment, tears of joy, or a racing heartbeat are all physical expressions of our inner emotional state. Conversely, tangible actions can evoke a profound emotional response. A warm embrace might bring comfort and security, while a harsh word can cause pain or anger. This interplay is essential to the human condition.

Our aspirations and dreams, though intangible, are powerful forces that direct our choices and the paths we take in life. The time we cherish with loved ones, the careers we choose, the hobbies we pursue—all are deeply influenced by these unseen motivators. Our formless ideas influence our actions and decisions long before they take shape in the physical world.

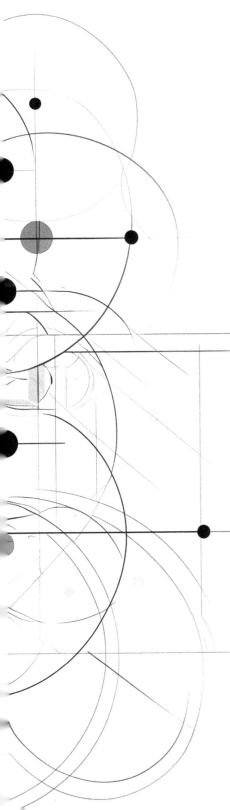

Art serves as a vivid illustration of this interplay. It allows us to express emotions and ideas that go beyond the physical. Whether it's through painting, music, or literature, art captures the essence of the intangible and transforms it into a tangible form, communicating the profound depths of human emotion and thought.

In the business world, the interplay of the tangible and intangible is equally pivotal. While concrete observations and calculations are crucial in decision-making, it is often our intuition, a subtle yet powerful guide, that helps us navigate through uncertainties.

The tangible aspects of a product or service are intertwined with intangible factors like customer service quality and brand perception, both of which significantly influence our emotional connection with a brand. Similarly, a company's culture affects employee morale and productivity, and its brand reputation can establish either consumer loyalty or aversion.

The interaction between the tangible and intangible is in constant flux, each shaping and redefining the other. While analysis of each separate element can be insightful, understanding their interconnectedness offers a more comprehensive view of our world. The tangible provides form to the intangible, while the intangible infuses the tangible with meaning and purpose. Recognizing and valuing this dynamic interplay enhances our understanding of the complexities and beauty of life, both personally and in the broader context of business and technology. This intricate, perpetual dance is at the very core of our existence.

THIS IS ALL VERY PERSONAL

For humans, the material world has long been our familiar terrain. During countless millennia, we've navigated its contours, assigning names to its myriad elements, and creating systems to measure and compare. The tangibility of this world lends itself to a semblance of control, an illusion of mastery. But beyond this lies a realm far more elusive, a domain of intangible elements where standard metrics falter and definitions blur.

This intangible world is not uncharted, but its exploration is akin to a child's first steps, tentative and unsteady. Numerous branches of science, such as psychology, philosophy, and even theoretical physics, have ventured into this realm. They probe abstractions like emotions, thoughts, and aspirations, seeking to understand and quantify what is beyond our touch. Nevertheless, our grasp of the immaterial remains, at best, embryonic, especially when compared to our extensive study of the physical world.

The intangible is inherently subjective, varying dramatically from one person to the next. Consider love, a concept universally acknowledged yet uniquely experienced. Or take beauty, the appreciation of which shifts not only between individuals but across cultures and epochs. These ideas resist standardization; they are fluid, shaped by personal experiences, cultural backgrounds, and temporal contexts.

Adding to the complexity, many of these intangible elements are in perpetual motion, thriving in a realm of abundance. They are not confined by the scarcity that often characterizes the physical world. For instance, knowledge and creativity know no bounds; they expand and evolve continuously, and often in unpredictable ways. Similarly, concepts like morality, ethics, and human rights are dynamic, continuously reinterpreted and redefined by society.

This constant state of flux makes discussion of the immaterial challenging. How do we quantify a feeling like hope, or a nebulous concept like wisdom?

HOW WOULD YOU PLACE THESE?

↑ **FEELS ABSTRACT**

← **SHARED**

PERSONAL →

↓ **FEELS CONCRETE**

Emotions

Thoughts

Faith   Beliefs

Spiritual convictions   Hope

Attitudes   Intuition

Identity

Ideas   Values

Ideals   Memories

Creativity

Morality   Wisdom

Knowledge

Loyalty   Legacy

Political ideoligies

Reputation   Charisma

Social norms

Digital twins   Omniverse   Brand   Trust

Data   Software   Commitment

Metaverse   Friendship

Artificial intelligence

Copyrights   Customs   Cultural practices

Contracts   History

Nation states   Companies   Religious doctrines

Laws   Patents

There is no one right answer here. These are difficult concepts to talk about in a business context. We often avoid such discussions, focusing instead on the tangible, which is easier to understand.

Equally abstract are constructs like social norms and cultural practices. Not only are they intangible but deeply rooted in collective human behavior and thought.

The realm of the intangible also extends to modern constructs like digital identities, cyber security, and AI. Though rooted in the material world of technology, they transcend physicality, shaping our perceptions, interactions, and reality in profound ways. The digital twin, the blockchain, and the metaverse are all concepts that straddle the line between the tangible and intangible, reshaping our appreciation of both.

In this journey of exploration, we find that our tools for understanding the material world fall short. We are left with more questions than answers. Perhaps that is the beauty of it. The intangible world, with its fluidity and subjectivity, invites a different kind of exploration—one that is not about conquest or control, but contemplation, understanding, and appreciation of the diverse experiences that make up the human condition.

A reminder for the author: This is a business book, not a cosmic exploration guide. It's intended for business leaders, strategists, and consultants, helping them to uncover new ideas and perspectives. Or, at least, to provide a slightly more engaging read during their toilet breaks. So, let's keep our corporate hat firmly in place. We're in business territory now!

As we delve deeper into this intangible realm, we learn that it is not about definitive answers or rigid frameworks. Instead, it's about embracing ambiguity, recognizing the diversity of experiences and perspectives, and continually adapting our understanding. In doing so, not only do we enrich our comprehension of the world, but we gain deeper insights into the nature of existence.

To recap, our perception of what's material and immaterial is deeply personal. This unique perspective is not a limitation, but a strength. It adds depth and originality to our understanding and creativity.

PLATO:

Imagine you see different chairs—a kitchen chair, a rocking chair, an office chair.* They all look different, right? But you still recognize them all as chairs. My Theory of Forms is about understanding why we can identify all these different objects as chairs, even though they're not exactly the same.

I believe there's a world that we can't see, a world of Forms or Ideas. In this world, there's a perfect version of everything we see around us. So, there's a perfect Form of a chair, a tree, a dog, beauty, goodness—you name it. These Forms are eternal, unchanging, and are the most real things that exist.

The chairs we see and sit on in our world are just copies or imitations of this perfect chair Form. They're not perfect, and they change and decay, but they're still chairs because they share something in common with the perfect Form of a chair.

So, when we recognize something as a chair, it's because, in our souls, we remember the perfect Form of the chair from the world of Forms. It's like our souls have seen the perfect versions of everything before we were born, and now we're just seeing the imperfect copies in the physical world.

The truest reality is not the physical objects we see around us, but rather the perfect, unchanging ideas or Forms that these objects are just imperfect copies of.

*) Office chairs were a bit different back in his time. But you probably get the point.

PROVOCATION:
THE BEAUTY OF NOT PREDICTING

DAVID ERHARD

Head of Community at Siemens with over 13 years of experience in the video game industry, including roles at Electronic Arts, Activision and King. Known for contributions to iconic brands such as EA Sports FIFA, Candy Crush, and Command & Conquer, leveraging a strong background in creative strategy.

IN an era dominated by analytics and profit margins, gaming and other creative industries find themselves at a critical juncture where a battle continues to rage. In one camp can be found the advocates of creative ingenuity, in the other are those drawn to the comforting security of predictability and commercial success. What is the impact of this conflict on the evolution and integrity of game design?

Historically, gaming was a domain of unbridled creativity. Passionate designers and developers, from a variety of backgrounds and crafts, shared a vision that inspired the creation of iconic games that were to endure for decades. These were more than products; they were experiences, meticulously crafted to offer something new and exciting. They offered narratives that pulled players in, immersing them in ways they had never experienced before with any other entertainment format.

Yet, such an approach has become increasingly rare in today's market. Now, financial calculations and marketability often dictate the direction of game development. Creators are often asked to assess the potential payoff before they can commit to exercising their creative muscles and realizing their vision.

The shift from innovation to monetization is most evident in the strategies employed by major gaming franchises. Once pioneers of creativity and engagement, they built some of our most beloved brands, including The Legend of Zelda, Prince of Persia, and Command & Conquer. Many of the companies behind these games now rely on iterative updates and microtransactions, prioritizing revenue over user experience. They forget that the beauty of these games—what drew me in as a kid—are their stories and the alternate worlds they give us to explore.

I have been on the other side of the fence, too. My studio colleagues and I had invested two years crafting a premium gaming experience when we were instructed to reorient the game towards a free-to-play model. This compromised its original vision for the sake of monetization and saw it rushed to market.

This trend is symptomatic of a broader issue within creative industries, from Hollywood filmmaking to television production to gaming. In the pursuit of surefire hits, there's a reluctance to invest in unproven, innovative ideas. Consequently, the market is flooded with sequels and remakes, leading to a homogenized landscape. This cautious approach not only limits the diversity of available films, shows, and games but also stifles the creative spirit of developers.

With the increased focus on profitability in gaming, there is a risk that games become less artistic and exploratory, serving instead as advertising platforms. This threatens to diminish the emotional and psychological satisfaction that players derive from the gaming experience. In short, it will kill the magic.

But not all hope is lost. The indie gaming scene remains a bastion of creativity and risk-taking. Unencumbered by the heavy expectations of shareholders, these smaller studios are free to experiment and innovate. Today, they are the source of truly unique and memorable gaming experiences. They remind us of the potential of gaming not just entertain, but to inspire and challenge.

It would be great to see some of their inventiveness and vitality creeping back into the major gaming studios—a return to a bolder vision, with more products developed simply because people see a need and believe. Hell, I'd love to see more humanity, creativity, and purpose-driven decision making in all business, not just gaming. With the advent of AI, this seems even more important than it did before.

Gaming has always been about creating imaginary universes with peculiar sets of laws and rules. Designers and developers have granted us access to these fantasy worlds—from simple board games to role-playing entertainments to massive online adventures. In the midst of another enormous technological revolution, we should be stepping beyond commercial and creative constraints, beyond predictive certainties, freeing ourselves to fantasize and create new immersive worlds that have the capacity to reshape the physical one we currently inhabit.

HISTORY OF THE INTANGIBLE

From scary spirits to the power of Wall Street and new levels of humanity.

HOW WE HAVE USED THE IMMATERIAL WORLD

From oral stories, myths, and religions to brands, digital identities, and virtual realities

Ⅰ Explain

Initially, the intangible world served a primarily explanatory purpose. People turned to it to give reasoning to phenomena in the real world that they couldn't otherwise comprehend. For instance, myths and legends about invisible creatures and mysterious places were crafted to understand and describe the unknown.

Ⅱ Control

As society evolved, the intangible world was harnessed to exert control over various aspects of the tangible world. This was achieved through the creation of abstract structures and mechanisms, such as clans, kingdoms, laws, and religions. These intangible concepts helped in organizing societies, establishing order, and set power structures.

At this moment, all these levels coexist. At home, people talk to angels, while at work they respond to machine learning predictions about future malware threats. The explanatory myths, controlling structures, rapid information dissemination, and replicative advancements of the intangible realm live side by side with the tangible.

WE ARE HERE

ⅢAccelerate

The immaterial domain has facilitated the rapid acceleration of information dissemination, learning, and networking. Technologies and platforms, from the printing press to the radio to the internet, have bridged gaps and created a more interconnected world, enhancing the speed at which we operate.

ⅣReplicate

Further advancements in technology have enabled us to create digital replicas or representations of the tangible world. This not only allows for simulations and modeling but for immersive experiences that blur the boundaries between the real and the virtual.

ⅤCreate

Here the intangible realm, combined with technologies like AI and artificial general intelligence (AGI), will be used to materialize both physical entities and novel intangible realms. In the future, the immaterial world won't just mirror or replicate reality, but actively shape and create it so that we will be unable to tell them apart.

During the prehistoric era—before humans were able to ask about the location of the nearest toilet—there were many greater questions that they grappled with. With the miracle of speech came the first inquiries about the great unknowns. Restroom directions followed long after. ●

As they learned to speak, people pondered the mysteries of nature. Why was it that on some occasions hunters enjoyed good fortune and on others they returned empty-handed? What happened to people when they died? And what the f*ck was that colorful arc that appeared in the sky?

Fortunately, the tribe had a wise man with all the answers. He was a creative fellow. He asserted that misfortune in hunting could be avoided by sacrificing food to the all-powerful hidden little folk. As for the deceased, they journeyed to a secret realm where eternal joy awaited them. And that colorful arc? It was said to be a bridge to a pot full of shiny treasure. Good luck finding it!

No scientific proof whatsoever. ● If you have no idea how something actually works, the best way to fill the gaps in your wisdom is with an intangible explanation. It's the perfect cover! No one can ever prove you wrong if you claim that the death of your pet wolf was because of bad karma or a curse.

EXPLAINING THE TANGIBLE THROUGH THE INTANGIBLE

During prehistoric times, people's knowledge of the surrounding world was limited. Often, beliefs, superstition, and supernatural forces—rather than facts and knowledge—accounted for difficult-to-understand phenomena and frightening events like volcanic eruptions, earthquakes, and solar eclipses.

The natural world was a vast, uncharted territory filled with mystery.

Ancient civilizations developed rich mythologies to explain these natural phenomena. In Egyptian mythology, the flooding of the Nile, essential for agriculture, was attributed to the tears of the goddess Isis. In Norse mythology, thunderstorms were believed to be the sound of Thor riding his chariot across the skies.

Early cultures also relied on shamans and medicine men/women/other who used intangible rituals, chants, and trance-like states to heal the sick or to scare off the mythical creatures stirring beneath the ground or devouring the sun. Shamans were revered figures who served as intermediaries between the living and the dead. They believed that the spirits of the deceased could offer guidance and protection.

In Siberia, for instance, shamans entered trance states, often induced by rhythmic drumming, to journey into the spirit world for guidance or healing. In Native American traditions, shamans used dream interpretation and animal totems to guide and protect their communities.

During the Middle Ages, alchemists sought to transform base metals into gold. This pursuit was not just about tangible experimentation but was deeply intertwined with mystical and spiritual beliefs.

Traditional medicine in various cultures relied on intangible concepts like the balance of humors or the power of herbs. Knowledge of medicinal properties was often passed down through generations.

Astrology, still practiced today, is an example of how celestial positions were used to explain and predict events on Earth. People believed that the position of stars and planets had a direct influence on human affairs.

Religions have depended on intangible beliefs to explain, influence, and shape the tangible world. Religion has been a powerful force in human history, providing both individual and societal frameworks for understanding the world and our place in it. To strengthen the connection with the otherworldly, the design of temples and other places of worship often incorporate sacred geometry to align these structures with the cosmos or the divine.

Intangible explanations, often rooted in spirituality and mysticism, were essential to early humans wanting to make sense of the tangible world. This reliance on intangible beliefs and practices has played a significant role in shaping cultures and societies for millennia. **It still does.**

THE INTANGIBLE AS A FORM OF CONTROL

The power of the intangible is formidable, often overshadowing the tangible. It is the power to shape belief, to mold perception, to direct the collective will. This power has been understood and harnessed throughout history by those who seek to govern not just the physical but also the ethereal aspects of human existence.

Religions have long recognized the potency of the intangible. Shamans, priests, and clerics, acting as intermediaries between the divine and the earthly, have leveraged their unique position to expand their influence. Through rituals, doctrines, and the promise of understanding the unknowable, religious leaders have secured a central role in their communities. They have been the custodians of sacred knowledge, the guardians of the unseen. In their hands, intangible spirituality has been transformed into powerful authority.

Monopolizing explanation of the unseen world, religious institutions not only have grown in social and political influence but also have accumulated material wealth. The intangible, in this sense, translates into very tangible outcomes. The power derived from the unseen has been used to construct vast edifices of religious, cultural, and social life, establishing a hierarchy where the few interpret the divine for the many.

The intangible threads of belief and doctrine have been spun into a web that supports the weight of churches, temples, and mosques—structures not just of stone and wood, but of power and prestige. This web extends into people's daily lives, influencing their choices, shaping their values, and dictating their place in the grand scheme of things.

In considering the role of the intangible in society, we must acknowledge

Now I get it! Lord Voldemort is the father of all these thoughts.

43

its double-edged nature. While the intangible can uplift and unify, it also can control and dominate. The invisible threads, when woven with wisdom and care, can create a society rich in spiritual and cultural fabric. Yet, when wielded with self-interest and greed, the same threads can bind and restrict, holding tight the reins of power.

As society's architects continue to pull and tighten these threads, the questions need to be asked not only about how they are used, but about who gets to hold them, and to what end. The exploration of these intangible threads leads us to the heart of power itself, revealing the structures that underpin our civilization and the forces that shape our collective destiny.

DIVINE CONNECTION

Throughout history, the divine connection has been a pivotal intangible thread used by rulers to weave their legitimacy and assert control over their subjects. There is evidence of the entanglement of religion and state across countless faiths, nations, and empires. With Christianity, for example, by declaring themselves as chosen by the divine, monarchs secured a form of power that was beyond the reach of any human contestation. This celestial endorsement served as an invisible crown, more powerful than any physical symbol of royalty.

The concept of the "divine right to rule" was not merely a statement of belief, it was a political doctrine, serving as a potent weapon that monarchs like England's James I used to engrain their sovereignty into the consciousness of their people. By asserting that their authority was granted by a higher power, monarchs placed themselves above human judgment and earthly accountability.

This doctrine was ingeniously self-reinforcing. The Church, which stood as the intermediary between the divine and the earthly, supported the monarch's claim to divine right. In doing so, it effectively placed itself at the heart of the power dynamics within the realm. It became the spiritual validator of the monarch's right to rule, which, in turn, elevated the Church's own position within society. The Church was solely responsible for interpreting sacred doctrine. It controlled the spiritual narrative, shaping the beliefs and behaviors of the populace and entrenching its own status within the societal hierarchy.

The relationship between the crown and the cross was symbiotic and strategic. The Church's backing of the monarch's divine right to rule was a show of support that often came with expectations—land grants, wealth, and influence. In exchange, the Church's doctrines were enshrined and protected by the power of the throne, creating a cycle of mutual reinforcement that was difficult to break.

In such a society, the intangible—the divine right, the sacred doctrines, the religious endorsement—transcended the tangible. It was not the strength of armies alone that maintained a monarch's rule, but the belief in their divine appointment. It was not the walls of the Church that gave it power, but the faith in its interpretation of the divine will.

THE USE OF DIVINE CONNECTION AS A TOOL FOR CONTROL UNDERSCORES THE IMMENSE POWER OF INTANGIBLE ELEMENTS IN SHAPING HUMAN SOCIETIES.

The use of divine connection as a tool for control underscores the immense power of intangible elements in shaping human societies. It illustrates how beliefs, when institutionalized and monopolized, can be woven into the very fabric of societal structures, influencing governance and societal norms. The divine right to rule, a thread spun from celestial narratives, effectively bound the subjects to their ruler. This went beyond mere loyalty, providing them with a sense of sacred duty and divine purpose.

) I'm focusing on European Christianity simply because it's the religion I'm most familiar with. Let's be honest, it's always easier to poke fun at what you know best. But don't worry, the principles I'm talking about are like a one-size-fits-all t-shirt; they apply to numerous other religions, too.

KNOWLEDGE IS POWER

In the annals of history, knowledge has consistently served as the cornerstone of power. The control of information—its creation and dissemination—has been a method employed by the few to maintain dominion over the many. There was a stark division between those who possessed knowledge and those who were deliberately kept in ignorance.

For centuries, literacy was not a universal right but a selective privilege. The literate were typically religious leaders, royalty, and a select group of scholars. This exclusive club used its command of language to shape the intellectual and spiritual discourse of their times.

The withholding of knowledge was a calculated strategy. By ensuring that literacy remained a luxury beyond the reach of the common people, the elite secured their position of power. They became the sole narrators of history, the only voices of authority, and the exclusive architects of the future. The pen, in their hands, was mightier than the sword, for it wrote the laws, the religious texts, and the philosophies that defined civilizations.

This manipulation of knowledge extended into the realm of education. The curricula taught to the few who were permitted to learn were carefully curated. Education systems, from the ancient to the modern, have often been wielded as tools of ideological influence, with authorities determining what should be taught, thereby shaping the intellectual and ethical contours of their citizens.

Seriously. Let's put some pictures in here! Tangible or immaterial, I don't care. Even the damn gorilla will do!

Even today, with widespread literacy, the control of knowledge remains a potent lever of power. The repositories of information have evolved from the ancient scriptoria to the vast digital databases of the modern era, but the principle remains unchanged. The guardians of information, whether institutions, governments, or corporations, have the ability to shape worldviews and influence the trajectory of societies.

The thread of knowledge, invisible yet foundational, is woven through the very fabric of society, acting as both a scaffold for progress and a barrier to it. As we consider the role of education and information in our world, we are reminded of its dual potential: to empower and to control.

IN TIMES OF CRISIS, WE ARE LED BY THE INTANGIBLE

Crises are the anvils upon which the intangible elements of power are hammered into shape. At such times, the invisible forces of ideology and belief come to the fore, mobilizing the masses. Nationalism, political doctrines, and narratives of historical destiny become tools for those seeking to consolidate or seize power.

Leaders, whether despotic or democratically elected, have long understood the utility of the intangible in rallying a nation. During moments of turmoil, they harness the collective spirit, drawing upon the shared beliefs, values, and aspirations of their people. They invoke the narratives of a group's illustrious past or presumed intellectual or moral superiority to forge a common identity, often in opposition to a designated other.

This unity is further solidified through the use of symbols and slogans, which serve as the embodiment of intangible ideologies. Flags are not merely cloth, but potent symbols of unity and resistance. Slogans and propaganda are more than words; they are the melodies to which the collective consciousness marches. These tools are wielded with precision to manipulate emotions and mold public opinion.

THE POWER OF THE INTANGIBLE IS MAGNIFIED IN TIMES OF CRISIS. WHEN THE FUTURE IS UNCERTAIN AND FEAR RUNS RAMPANT, THE ALLURE OF A STRONG NARRATIVE THAT OFFERS A SENSE OF PURPOSE, HOPE, AND DIRECTION IS IRRESISTIBLE.

The power of the intangible is magnified in times of crisis. When the future is uncertain and fear runs rampant, the allure of a strong narrative that offers a sense of purpose, hope, and direction is irresistible. Leaders who effectively utilize these intangible tools can secure their authority and guide the collective will of the people.

Leaders' use of the intangible during times of crisis is a dance as ancient as society itself—a testament to the enduring power of ideas, beliefs, and emotions in shaping human action. The narratives we cling to, the symbols we revere, and the slogans we chant become the threads that hold us together when the world seems to be unraveling.

As we reflect on the role of the intangible during crises, we see a pattern of mobilization and control. Invisible elements are powerful precisely because they tap into the core of human identity and emotion. They are the compass points by which societies, for better or worse, navigate stormy seas and uncertain times.

SOCIETIES WITH STRONG INTANGIBLE STRUCTURES

As architects of society, governments and bureaucracies function not just in the realm of the physical but are deeply entrenched in the intangible. They are the custodians of abstract constructs such as taxation, property rights, and legal frameworks, which they translate into the concrete mechanisms that govern public life. This translation from the intangible to the tangible is critical in shaping the day-to-day experiences of individuals within a society.

The systems established by such entities provide a semblance of order and predictability. These systems, however, are double-edged swords. On one hand, they create a structure within which society can function smoothly; on the other, they often cement the power structures, inadvertently benefiting those who are already at the helm. The rules and regulations, while essential for order, can sometimes reinforce the status quo, making it challenging for others.

In the invisible structures of society, values such as justice and order are intangible yet are reflected in the very tangible form through laws and regulations. Courts and legal codes do not merely enforce laws, they reflect a society's moral compass, upholding its ideals and maintaining the balance of power. These institutions support the authority of those in power, sometimes at the expense of the marginalized, perpetuating long-standing power dynamics.

However, in democratic systems, the intangible structure of power division—executive, legislative, and judicial—serves a different purpose. It creates checks and balances that provide predictability and security, enabling individuals to have the agency to act freely within the parameters of the law. This tripartite division is designed to prevent the concentration of power and to ensure that no single entity can become too dominant.

This division of power is an intangible concept that has tangible effects on the freedoms and rights of individuals. It forms the backbone of democratic societies, providing a framework within which freedom and agency can flourish. The effectiveness of these intangible structures lies in their ability to be internalized and respected by those whom they govern.

The role of intangible structures in society is as crucial as the physical infrastructures that support our cities and towns. They are the unseen forces that give shape to our social order, the silent codes that govern our interactions, and the quiet guidelines that inform our freedoms and responsibilities.

These structures provide the steps that societies follow, often unconsciously, as they move through the complexities of modern life. While this process can result in harmony, it requires constant vigilance to ensure that it remains a dance of equity and not one of oppression.

THE JOURNEY CONTINUES ●

In the vast ocean of contemporary society, the currents of power have shifted with the tide of data. This intangible force, no longer manifesting as myth or monarchy, has emerged as bytes and bandwidth. Data, the lifeblood of the digital age, now forms the domain where corporate entities exert their influence, shaping the marketplace and consumer behavior.

Today's tech titans have seized control of this potent but unseen force. With extensive data at their disposal, they navigate the economic seas, sculpting consumer realities. Their power is not demonstrated through traditional symbols like scepters but through algorithms, not declared from high platforms but subtly integrated into software codes and internet pathways.

Data's influence is both omnipresent and imperceptible. It guides what we see online, the ads that draw our attention, and the content that molds our views. It directs not only economic markets but social interaction itself. Consumer data mirrors our desires, fears, and preferences, all while being shaped by those who collect it.

Today, power and control are less about direct domination and more about understanding and predicting behavior. Tech giants have honed this skill, converting intangible data into tangible profits, transforming user behavior into predictable trends.

This newfound power carries responsibilities and risks. The misuse of data casts a long shadow across the digital realm. As society becomes more aware of data's intangible value, greater importance is given to privacy, consent, and ethical use.

●
OMG, the Journey continues. This is going to end badly. Very badly.

Navigating power in the digital age is complex and nuanced. It demands a careful balance between leveraging data's potential and respecting the intangible aspects of human privacy and autonomy. The course we chart now will set the direction of our future interactions in the marketplace and beyond.

THE INTANGIBLE AS
AN ACCELERATOR

Intangible factors have a multiplier effect on every aspect of human progress, from how we form communities to how we evolve and perceive our place in the universe.

INFORMATION

The trajectory of human advancement has been firmly linked to the dissemination of knowledge. Since Johannes Gutenberg invented the printing press, moving from calfskin to paper, we've witnessed an unprecedented democratization of information. This shift not only changed who could access it but also how rapidly it could spread.

Early information dissemination was largely controlled by the elite—academics, clerics, and the wealthy. However, the emergence of educational institutions, libraries, newspapers, magazines, and later radio and television, catalyzed a phenomenal triumph of knowledge-sharing. This evolution embodies the transition from knowledge as a privileged commodity to a universally accessible resource.

Sir Francis Bacon's adage, "knowledge is power," rings truer than ever in our current age. However, the nature of this power has undergone a transformative shift.

Up until the mid-20th century, acquiring in-depth knowledge often required access to specific physical locations, such as universities or corporate research departments. This inevitably limited who could participate in innovation and research.

The internet has radically altered this landscape. No longer tethered to physical locations or mediums, information now exists in an ethereal, almost omnipresent state. The intangible nature of information, once constrained by physical and social limitations, has been fully realized in the digital age. This liberation of information has exponentially accelerated our capacity for innovation, allowing a far wider demographic to contribute to and benefit from collective human intelligence.

The intangible quality of knowledge, inherently non-physical but immensely powerful, becomes a profound accelerator in our world. It is the driving force behind rapid advancements in technology, society, and individual empowerment. As information becomes more accessible, the collective human potential expands, leading to advancements in fields ranging from science to the arts.

This democratization of information marks a decisive moment in human history. It signifies not just a technological revolution but a cultural and intellectual awakening. The power once held by a select few is now dispersed, igniting a global, collaborative effort toward progress and innovation.

In essence, the world of information and knowledge acts not just as a repository of facts and figures but as a dynamic, ever-evolving catalyst for human growth and societal transformation. As we continue to explore and understand this intangible realm, we unlock new possibilities for our collective future.

COMPANIES

Throughout history, humanity has conceived various intangible constructs, yet few have spurred development as significantly as the concept of companies, particularly limited liability companies. The LLC structure represents a pivotal innovation in the business world, fundamentally altering the landscape of corporate responsibility and risk.

The genius of the LLC lies in its ability to separate personal liability from corporate actions. This means that the individuals involved

THE GENIUS OF THE LLC LIES IN ITS ABILITY TO SEPARATE PERSONAL LIABILITY FROM CORPORATE ACTIONS

are not personally liable for the company's financial losses or debts. In scenarios involving legal challenge or business failure, it is the company, as an independent entity, that bears the brunt of liability, not employees, partners, or shareholders. This separation of personal and corporate liability has profound implications for business operations and risk-taking.

While natural evolution typically unfolds through gradual adaptations and the survival of the fittest, it also undergoes significant shifts and transformations. A parallel can be drawn in the corporate world. Here, the agility of LLCs becomes crucial. Their capacity for rapid adaptation to market shifts, technological breakthroughs, and evolving consumer demands is a standout feature. This dynamic, characterized by periods of intense change and innovation, is vital for a company's survival. In a marketplace where the inability to evolve can be fatal, the evolutionary agility of LLCs is not just advantageous but essential for their continued existence.

This heightened competition fosters a hotbed of innovation. LLCs are incentivized to develop new products, services, and processes to gain an edge over competitors. This constant innovation cycle leads to remarkable technological and procedural advancements, contributing significantly to overall economic growth and societal progress.

The pace at which LLCs move is extraordinary. The lifecycle of products, business models, and market strategies is much shorter compared to earlier times. This rapid pace demands agility and a forward-thinking approach from businesses, leading to a dynamic economic environment where change is the only constant.

The intangible nature of LLCs, while fostering economic growth and innovation, also raises critical questions about corporate responsibility and the long-term impact of business activities on the planet. The challenge lies in balancing the drive for development and profit with a sustainable approach that respects and preserves the natural world. This balance is crucial for ensuring that the immense potential of LLCs as accelerators of human progress does not come at an unsustainable ecological cost.

DATA

The transformative role of computers in propelling the intangible world into a new era of progress cannot be overstated. However, it was the accumulation and strategic utilization of data that truly unleashed the potential of these digital marvels. Data, in its vast and varied forms, has become a fundamental asset in driving innovation, foresight, and efficiency across multiple domains.

One of the most tangible impacts of data accumulation is the ability to "travel in time," metaphorically speaking. Through predictive analytics, we can forecast future events with remarkable accuracy. Weather prediction is a prime example. By analyzing historical and real-time data, meteorological models can accurately predict weather patterns, effectively allowing us a glimpse into the future. This predictive capability extends beyond weather to numerous fields, including finance, healthcare, and logistics, where forecasting can lead to more informed decision-making and proactive strategies.

AI

The advent of large language models (LLMs) and AI applications marks a significant milestone in the journey of data utilization. These models, trained on vast pools of data, represent the first widely commercialized application of artificial intelligence. They exemplify how data, when harnessed effectively, can create systems that not only process information but also generate new content, solve complex problems, and provide insights that were previously inaccessible.

These AI systems, fueled by expansive datasets, are revolutionizing creativity and productivity. They enable people to enhance and supplement their skills, augmenting the capacity for what can be achieved regardless of temporal, spatial, linguistic, or capability constraints. For organizations, AI systems can serve as repositories of information and amplifiers of collective knowledge, enhancing decision-making and operational efficiency.

The integration of AI into various sectors is creating an unparalleled wave of creativity and productivity. From automating routine tasks to generating novel ideas and solutions, AI systems are enabling a higher level of performance and innovation. This is not just about replacing human effort but rather augmenting and extending it. Individuals and organizations can leverage AI to tackle more complex challenges, explore new possibilities, and achieve goals that were previously out of reach.

INTANGIBLE REPLICAS
OF THE MATERIAL WORLD

The dawn of the digital era marked a paradigm shift, transforming how we perceive and interact with our world. The inception of computers, followed by the development of software, data processing, and the internet, has ushered in an age where the intangible has become as real and influential as the physical. This transition to a digital world is not just a technological leap, it's a fundamental change in the very fabric of society and culture.

SOUNDS OF DIGITALIZATION

The music industry stands as a prime example of this transformation. The journey from live performances to recorded music encapsulates the shift from the tangible to the intangible. Initially, music was an experience, ephemeral and bound to time and place. Recording technology allowed the artist's skill to be captured and replicated, detaching the music from the performer. With the advent of digital technology, music took on a new form, from grooves and tapes to binary codes on compact discs, and eventually to data streams accessible via the internet. This last transition, while seemingly incremental, had profound implications for artists and the industry. The economic model, based on the distribution of physical media, had to be rethought as music became a digital commodity, flowing freely over the internet.

The transformation witnessed in the music industry was just the beginning. Numerous sectors underwent similar changes. News organizations, travel agencies, and retail stores, to name a few, have all embraced digital counterparts to their physical entities. Human interaction, once predominantly face-to-face, has shifted to digital platforms. The rise of social media, blockchain technology, digital banking, and e-wallets is a testament to this shift. Digitalization has not resulted in the replacement of physical objects and spaces but has augmented them with intangible, digital versions.

DATA LAYER

There is a dynamic, intricate web interwoven with our physical world that enhances, interprets, and in some cases, controls it. Today, each device we use, every structure we build, and the multitude of digital interactions we engage in, all contribute to the data layer. This interconnected network is more than a repository of information; it's a living, breathing digital ecosystem. The proliferation of sensors, cameras, and other data-gathering devices has made this layer incredibly detailed and accurate, mirroring the physical world in real-time.

One of the most significant advancements within the data layer is the concept of "digital twins." These digital replicas of physical systems allow for elaborate simulations in various settings, from industrial plants to complex infrastructures like airports. An airport's digital twin, for example, offers a comprehensive, interactive model of its entire ecosystem. It encompasses everything from passenger flow and baggage handling to security protocols and flight operations. By simulating and analyzing these complex interactions, airport management can anticipate issues, streamline operations, and enhance the passenger experience. This digital mirroring effectively transforms an airport from a mere physical space into a highly efficient, responsive organism, capable of adapting to the ever-changing demands of air travel. It allows stakeholders to collaborate more effectively, sharing insights and data, enabling proactive management of this multifaceted environment. The benefits are manifold, including improved safety, increased operational efficiency, and the potential for significant cost savings.

Beyond specific applications like airports, digital twins in industrial settings optimize processes and solve problems in the digital realm before the implementation of physical changes. This extends to digitally constructing and testing entire production lines or new plants, significantly reducing costs and risks associated with physical experimentation.

While the data layer brings immense benefits in terms of optimization and efficiency, it also raises concerns. The level of surveillance and data collection involved can be seen as dystopian, especially in societies where privacy and personal freedom are paramount. The balance between leveraging this digital layer for societal benefits while safeguarding individual rights is a delicate one.

ENVISIONING THE METAVERSE

The metaverse represents a collective dream of a virtual environment where human interaction, creativity, and experience are not limited by the constraints of the physical world. It's envisioned as a boundless space where the lines between the real and the virtual blur, offering opportunities for immersive experiences far beyond what is currently possible. This vision includes a world where people can engage in activities, socialize, work, and create in ways that, at present, we can only imagine.

Despite the compelling vision of the metaverse, there are significant technological challenges and form factors that currently prevent the realization of a fully immersive virtual world. The quest for creating an all-encompassing virtual reality involves overcoming limitations in hardware, software, and network capabilities. However, the progress in this field is ongoing, and while a complete metaverse experience may still be some way off, advancements are steadily being made.

Precursors to the metaverse are clearly evident in the way we interact with technology today. Social media platforms, especially among younger generations, have begun to resemble a form of virtual world. These platforms, accessible via smartphones and computers, offer a space where the constraints of time and place are significantly diminished. Here, interactions occur through text, images, videos, and games, creating a rich tapestry of communication and expression that transcends physical and temporal boundaries.

THE EVOLUTION OF TRUTH

The digital era has revolutionized how we access news and information. Gone are the days when a handful of news outlets held sway, operating within defined journalistic standards. The advent of social media has

Is this the place where people have no legs? Now I understand what you mean by *immaterial*.

democratized information, leading to a proliferation of news sources. This abundance has led to a situation where "truth" is no longer a fixed entity but has become fluid, shaped by a myriad of perspectives.

Each individual now has the power to select their sources of information, effectively choosing their version of reality. This also has resulted in the phenomenon of echo chambers, where individuals or groups only engage with information that reinforces their pre-existing beliefs and perspectives. The result is a fragmented society, where shared objective realities seem to be fading away.

Digital platforms, particularly social media, play a crucial role in this new landscape. They are not just passive conduits of information but actively shape narratives through algorithms and corporate policies that determine what content is seen by whom. These platforms have become the new public squares, but ones subject to biased information dissemination.

REDUCED RESOURCE CONSUMPTION

Our economic model is built on the illusion of perpetual growth. Recently, however, a major shift has seen companies turn their attention to digital solutions. The digital transformation harbors significant environmental benefits. Rather than depleting finite material resources to fuel growth, companies can now expand in the boundless realm of the digital, where intangible assets reign.

It's important to acknowledge that digital services aren't devoid of tangible resource consumption. Server farms, for instance, are voracious consumers of electricity, needed both for operation and cooling. Additionally, the production of electronic components often requires rare earth metals.

Yet, the alternative—a reliance on physical resources for growth—would likely inflict far greater environmental harm. By embracing digital pathways, companies can mitigate the impact that their expansion would otherwise have on the physical world.

The digital layer, with its myriad sensors and data streams, has enabled more efficient use of resources in various sectors. In industrial environments, digital twins allow for the optimization of production processes, reducing waste and increasing efficiency. Smart city initiatives, leveraging IoT

(Internet of Things) technologies, optimize everything from traffic flow to energy use, significantly lowering the carbon footprint of urban areas.

The growth of digital technologies has paralleled the rise of renewable energy sources. The efficiency and optimization offered by digital solutions are instrumental in managing and distributing renewable energy more effectively. Smart grids, for example, use digital technology to optimize the distribution of electricity, integrating renewable sources like solar and wind more seamlessly.

THE EASE OF ACCESS

One of the paradoxical effects of digitalization is its potential to drive increased consumption. With data collection becoming more sophisticated, marketing becomes highly targeted, often stimulating consumer desires and demands. E-commerce platforms, combined with the convenience of instant home deliveries, have made shopping an almost effortless undertaking. This ease of access, while beneficial in many ways, can also lead to a surge in consumerism and, consequently, a rise in the production of goods, often at the expense of environmental sustainability.

The vast accumulation of data and the widespread monitoring of physical actions present significant privacy challenges. In an era where our digital footprints are constantly tracked and analyzed, concerns about data misuse and surveillance have become more pronounced. This surveillance can be exploited by various actors, ranging from criminals seeking personal information for fraudulent purposes to governments using data for oppressive control.

IMPACT ON TRADITIONAL INDUSTRIES AND LIVELIHOODS

Digitalization has drastically altered the landscape of many traditional industries, leading to the obsolescence of certain jobs and businesses. Industries that relied heavily on physical products and services have been hit particularly hard. For many workers, the shift to a digital-first economy has been challenging, with some struggling to adapt their skills to the new demands of the job market. This has led to economic disparities and challenges in ensuring equitable access to the opportunities presented by the digital age.

NEW INTANGIBLE DIMENSIONS

I n technology, innovations such as blockchain, DAOs, cryptocurrencies, and non-fungible tokens (NFTs) stand out as new examples of the intangible. We should not forget, too, that social media is relatively young and continues to play a role in changing human interaction and existence.

The advent of internet technology has not just bridged distances but has opened an entirely new dimension: the intangible digital world, which exercises an incredible draw on us.

Global statistics reveal that we spend about 44% of our waking hours engaged with screens. In the United States, children aged between 11 and 14 are the most voracious, averaging around nine hours a day. This statistic is a testament to the profound impact of the digital dimension on our daily lives, spanning professional work, gaming, entertainment, social interaction, and the huge amounts of time spent scrolling through news and social media feeds.

Did you doomscroll before it was cool?

The COVID-19 pandemic acted as a catalyst, accelerating the transition to digital platforms for work and collaboration. The necessity to work remotely taught us that it was both feasible and efficient to operate entirely within this intangible dimension.

However, the rapid migration from the tangible to the intangible also has affected physical wellbeing, social interaction, and community structures. Absorption by this digital realm often leads to a reduction in physical activity and face-to-face social engagements, raising concerns about long-term health and social skills.

In this digital era, concepts like reputation, trust, and ethics have gained new meanings. Traditional notions of privacy and identity are being redefined by digital identities and online communities. The digital landscape has become a breeding ground for innovative business models and organizational cultures.

BUT THIS IS JUST THE BEGINNING...

Our intangible world will experience a cycle of exponential evolution. These are just some of the changes awaiting us in the very near future:

Blending of worlds

The concept of virtual reality (VR), though not yet fully realized, stands on the brink of a transformative breakthrough. The future of VR is not one where individuals are confined to dark rooms, wearing cumbersome headsets. Instead, we are moving toward an era where the physical and digital worlds merge seamlessly, blurring the lines between what is real and what is virtual. This confluence will create a hybrid reality where digital enhancements enrich our physical experiences, making the transition between worlds fluid and natural.

Immaterial companions

Artificial Intelligence (AI) is poised to revolutionize our personal interactions. Imagine AI-powered companions tailored to understand and adapt to our unique personalities and needs. These companions could range from temporary assistants, aiding us in specific tasks or locations, to long-term sidekicks who evolve with us, learning and enhancing their understanding. The potential for AI to provide personalized, context-sensitive companionship is a profound shift in how we perceive and interact with technology.

These AI entities will possess a form of emotional intelligence, allowing them to recognize and respond to human emotions appropriately. This capability will enable them to provide companionship that feels genuine and responsive, rather than robotic and programmed.

Just like any relationship, the bond with an AI companion will develop over time. These AI systems will learn from each interaction, adapting their responses and behavior to better align with people's personalities and lives. This learning ensures that AI companions will remain relevant and supportive over an extended period.

New ways of thinking

As we generate and interact with vast amounts of data, both tangible and intangible, the need for more advanced computing power becomes crucial. Quantum computing has emerged as the solution, offering increased processing capabilities, as well as a new paradigm in computing. Unlike classical computing, which relies on bits (ones and zeroes), quantum computing uses qubits. Qubits can exist in multiple states simultaneously, thanks to quantum superposition. This allows quantum computers to process a vast number of possibilities at once, significantly outperforming traditional computers. This leap in computing power is essential for handling the complex, data-intensive tasks of our evolving digital world.

THE FUTURE: A DYNAMIC, SELF-CREATING WORLD

Combining these technologies—virtuality, AI, and quantum computing— we stand on the cusp of a dynamic new world, constantly recreating itself. The future will see technology integrated so seamlessly into our lives that it is no longer perceived as a separate entity. Gadgets, computers, mobile phones, and server farms will evolve into an all-encompassing technological ecosystem, intertwined with every aspect of our existence.

WHAT DOES THIS MEAN FOR BUSINESSES AND LEADERS?

This is not about digitizing your business. Instead, it signals a transformative shift in how companies operate, create value, and interact with customers and employees. Understanding and adapting to these changes will be crucial for businesses to thrive in this evolving landscape.

For business leaders and strategists, educating themselves about new technologies and their implications is no longer optional, it's a critical necessity. Understanding the nuances is essential for making informed decisions. Leaders must not only grasp the technical aspects but also the societal and ethical implications these technologies entail. Continuous learning will help leaders envision the future of business in a world where the intangible plays a pivotal role.

As AI makes employees more efficient, companies face a strategic choice: where to direct this newfound efficiency. This decision hinges on

empathy

I redacted this to give you some time to think. Take five minutes. Don't take out your smartphone. Think. What does this all mean for business leaders?

hope

care

love

success.

PROVOCATION:
THE DAWN OF ABUNDANT CREATIVITY

ALBERTO-GIOVANNI BUSETTO

Swiss-Italian AI executive, scientist, and investor. As the inaugural global head of Data & AI at both Merck Healthcare and The Adecco Group, Alberto led the creation and management of intelligent products in pharma, biotech, electronics, and employment.
He earned his doctorate from ETH Zürich, and has served on the faculty at the University of California, Santa Barbara.

Through human history, creativity has been understood to be a finite resource, a spark of genius flickering in the minds of the few. Generative artificial intelligence (GenAI) marks a paradigm shift, ushering in an era where creativity is not exclusive to humans with specific skills, education, or resources.

GenAI has the potential to make creativity abundant, providing tools for anyone with a vision. This shift is not only about the democratization of creativity, but of new and diverse forms of creation, which exceeds the collective creative potential of all humans.

As we explore the capabilities, limitations, and implications of GenAI when integrated in various aspects of life, we find ourselves entangled in an uncontrolled experiment. This has been driven by a combination of enthusiasm, economic incentives, and curiosity.

In its ability to recombine ideas and formulate them in novel ways, GenAI can simulate aspects of human creativity. AI systems can (re)produce artistic, musical, and literary content, as well as complex ideas, even outsmarting mathematicians when solving combinatorics problems. [1]

Unlike traditional software, which is programmed to follow specific rules, GenAI learns from existing data and is able to generalize and reproduce patterns learned from it. When supplemented by reinforcement learning, it can evolve continuously, mimicking aspects of human experiential learning.

GenAI also exceeds human creativity in several profound ways:

1. Volume & speed: It can generate in seconds what it would take someone days or weeks to create. This exponential increase in output leads to a sheer abundance of creative works.

2. Radical diversity & exploration: AI is not constrained by human biases or evolutionary necessities. Algorithmic models, such as transformers, can explore a vast array of styles, genres, and ideas, many of which might never have been conceived by human minds. This opens a multidimensional space of creative possibilities where imagination presents the only limitation.

3. Active collaborative creation: AI acts as an active collaborator, not just a passive tool. Creators can interact with AI, leading to novel and unexpected creations resulting from structured yet liberating interactions between many individuals.

GENAI HAS THE POTENTIAL TO MAKE CREATIVITY ABUNDANT, PROVIDING TOOLS FOR ANYONE WITH A VISION.

4. Personalization: GenAI can tailor content to individual tastes or needs, making creative works more relevant and personal than ever before.

The intersection of computational creativity and algorithmic information theory raises profound philosophical questions. It challenges our understanding of creativity as a uniquely human trait and invites us to reconsider the nature of innovation in the algorithmic age. As we explore the capabilities of large language models (LLMs) and delve deeper into computational creativity, we stand on the brink of a new frontier.

WHAT ARE THE STRATEGIC IMPLICATIONS FOR BUSINESS?

Democratization of Creativity

Creativity becomes a universal skill accessible to anyone, not just a select few with specific talents or resources.

Defining Creativity

Organizations are prompted to reevaluate the meaning of creativity within their context, deciding whether it's tied to individual genius or a collective, corporate effort.

Shift to Curation & Quality

With an overflow of creative content, the focus shifts from sheer creation to the curation of high-quality, impactful work. Businesses and creators alike must emphasize uniqueness and relevance to stand out.

Humans First

A shift towards creating unique, engaging user experiences and building communities. Success hinges on interactive and immersive experiences, leveraging collective intelligence through technology.

Innovation in IP Models

The challenge to traditional intellectual property models necessitates innovation in perceptions of creativity ownership, adapting to the collaborative and fluid nature of GenAI-driven creativity.

New Competitors

Level playing field allow individuals and small entities to compete with large organizations, potentially emerging as new competitors from unexpected quarters.

This is a realm where creativity is not just an artistic endeavor but an algorithmic one, where the complexity of ideas and their expressions are bound only by the limits of our computational capabilities and mathematical imagination. In this world, algorithmic systems are collaborators in the creative process, redefining the very essence of what it means to create.

REVOLUTION

The steam engine was the poster child of the Industrial Revolution. Today, the content engine is its analog.

The steam engine enabled mass production, turning artisanal and manual processes into automated, efficient systems. It marked a transition from limited, labor-intensive production to an era of abundance in physical goods. This shift not only boosted productivity but also redefined economic structures, labor markets, and even societal norms. It paved the way for modern capitalism and industrial economies. Its digital equivalent is found in the content engines powered by AI. They are doing for information, creativity, and education what the steam engine did for physical labor:

Content engines can generate vast amounts of material at a pace and volume unimaginable a few decades ago. This marks a shift from scarcity to abundance in digital and creative assets, entailing the mass production of content. Just as the steam engine made manufacturing accessible to many, content engines make creation accessible to a wider audience, regardless of technical skills or artistic training.

We have reached a new frontier in our relationship with technology. This will affect the global economy, as well as our own human nature. GenAI is not just a technological advancement, but the instigator of a cultural and creative revolution that will deliver abundance. It heralds a future where creativity is almost limitless, where most individuals can become creators, and where collective creativity becomes possible at scale.

This is the dawn of abundant creativity, of a world where the intangible becomes abundant in ways we are only just beginning to comprehend.

THE STEAM ENGINE WAS THE POSTER CHILD OF THE INDUSTRIAL REVOLUTION. TODAY, THE CONTENT ENGINE IS ITS ANALOG.

[1] https://www.nature.com/articles/d41586-023-04043-w

71

Finally, we get to the stuff that really matters! This part is for all the business leaders, wannabe leaders, strategists, and consultants. Now pay attention!

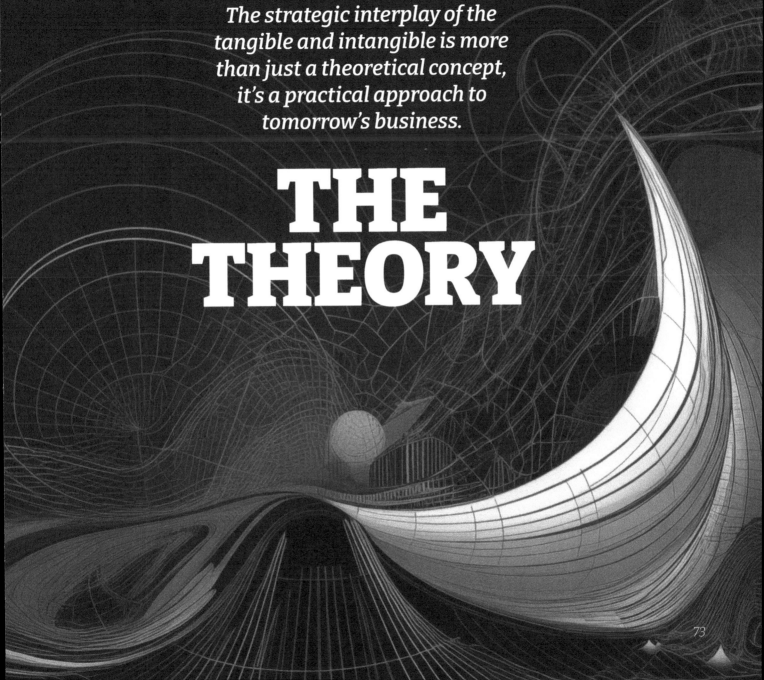

The strategic interplay of the tangible and intangible is more than just a theoretical concept, it's a practical approach to tomorrow's business.

THE THEORY

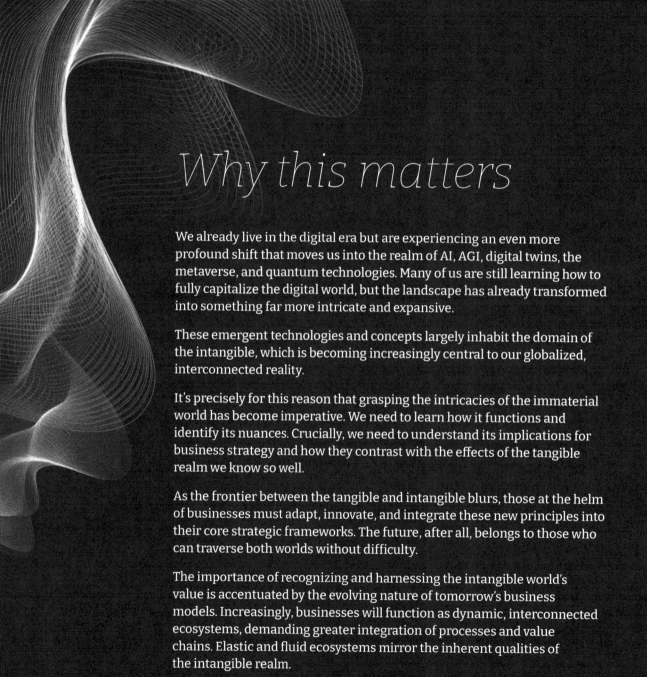

Why this matters

We already live in the digital era but are experiencing an even more profound shift that moves us into the realm of AI, AGI, digital twins, the metaverse, and quantum technologies. Many of us are still learning how to fully capitalize the digital world, but the landscape has already transformed into something far more intricate and expansive.

These emergent technologies and concepts largely inhabit the domain of the intangible, which is becoming increasingly central to our globalized, interconnected reality.

It's precisely for this reason that grasping the intricacies of the immaterial world has become imperative. We need to learn how it functions and identify its nuances. Crucially, we need to understand its implications for business strategy and how they contrast with the effects of the tangible realm we know so well.

As the frontier between the tangible and intangible blurs, those at the helm of businesses must adapt, innovate, and integrate these new principles into their core strategic frameworks. The future, after all, belongs to those who can traverse both worlds without difficulty.

The importance of recognizing and harnessing the intangible world's value is accentuated by the evolving nature of tomorrow's business models. Increasingly, businesses will function as dynamic, interconnected ecosystems, demanding greater integration of processes and value chains. Elastic and fluid ecosystems mirror the inherent qualities of the intangible realm.

A

As many businesses incorporate the intangible into their strategic thinking, the dynamics of what we understand as "mass" and "motion" undergo a radical shift. Traditional elements bound by physical properties are heavy, often requiring significant resources and energy to produce, manipulate, or transport. Contrast this with intangibles, which are devoid of mass, operating in an entirely different realm.

Digital products—whether apps, software, or cloud-based services—illustrate this transformation. Once developed, they can be replicated and distributed at a minimal incremental cost, reaching global audiences almost instantaneously. Their scalability is astounding. It's a far cry from the physical world, where producing more requires more raw materials, more labor, and more time.

However, the immaterial world is not just about absence of mass or the speed of propagation. It's about perpetual transformation. Intangibles don't merely "move," they morph, evolve, and interact in complex ways. This fluidity means they're never static, always reshaping, merging, splitting, and creating newer versions of themselves. Such boundless dynamism points to an abundant universe in which possibilities multiply exponentially.

But with abundance come challenges. Businesses, traditionally structured around concepts of control, ownership, and stability, find themselves in uncharted waters. In a realm where everything is in constant flux, how do we control or own anything? Traditional strategies centered on containment or monopoly struggle in this boundless space. Instead, success could hinge on adaptability, collaboration, and the ability to ride the wave of change rather than attempting to anchor it.

Wow, and now a physics lesson. How I hated them in school.

This transformative abundance of the immaterial world necessitates a rethink of business paradigms. As we venture deeper, the companies that will thrive are those that understand and harness its power while also navigating its unpredictability with agility and foresight.

THE INTERNET AS FIRESTARTER

The intangible domain has undergone a profound and revolutionary transformation during the past three decades. An increasing number of devices— and people who use them—have been connected to the internet, a vast and sprawling network of networks. The rate and scale of change within this immaterial sphere are unparalleled in its history.

While we consider data and software to be intangible, they differ significantly from abstract concepts like social norms, the narratives we share, and the notion of time itself.

Many of us recall the pre-internet era's computers: bulky, droning machines with limited capabilities. Transferring information then was a tangible process, involving the physical exchange of floppy disks.

As connectivity increased, data began to "take flight," moving across the globe with ease. This newfound fluidity became a disruptive force for industries that had previously relied on physical barriers to regulate information flow.

The surge in computing power, coupled with the shift to cloud storage, has accelerated the tempo of this change. Concurrently, numerous sectors have experienced swift digitization.

Today, virtually all new devices are equipped with microprocessors, and many are internet-enabled, ranging from the jewelry we wear to the automated lawn mowers in our gardens. Sectors as varied as finance, healthcare, and transportation, along with everyday objects like cars and health monitors, now generate and amalgamate data, impacting both our physical reality and the intangible aspects of our lives.

The digital sphere has evolved from isolated and localized systems into expansive, global data streams with increasingly intangible attributes.

Digitalization has given rise to novel intangible entities. For example, emerging forms of contracts, currencies, and advanced analytical methods to process and interpret large datasets were once outside the realm of possibility.

The internet, initially devised as a tool for exchanging information, has metamorphosed into a multifaceted platform that transcends its original purpose. It's not just about sharing information. The internet has become a canvas for human expression in all its forms. Our emotions, creative endeavors, and even our identities find a digital echo, resonating across the globe. This evolution has not only given birth to novel industries and professions but also cultivated unique cultures and communities. The internet now reflects our collective human experience, continually evolving and expanding the boundaries of the intangible world.

In this age of rapid technological advancement, we have witnessed the birth of new intangible elements that are reshaping our understanding of and interaction with the world.

DIGITAL RIPPLE EFFECTS

In the era of digital transformation, the traditional boundaries that once defined our business operations are being reshaped continuously. The digital realm, often misconceived as a separate entity, is an intricate mesh of tangible and intangible elements. This blending represents more than a mere evolution—it symbolizes a revolution in how we perceive, operate, and derive value from our business ventures.

Traditional business models often segregate operations into tangible and intangible categories. Physical assets, supply chains, and brick-and-mortar infrastructures are juxtaposed with concepts like brand value, intellectual property, and digital platforms. But the digital realm acts as a conduit, bridging these once-distinct worlds. Software, though intangible at its core, can catalyze the manufacture of a physical product. Conversely, tangible assets, like machinery, can be optimized through the use of digital twins, demonstrating the seamless interplay between the two realms.

As the lines blur, the value proposition of businesses is also undergoing a transformation. The worth of a company is no longer just about its physical assets and bottom line but also its digital footprint, data repositories, and

More intangible

When elements become more immaterial they present more of these qualities.

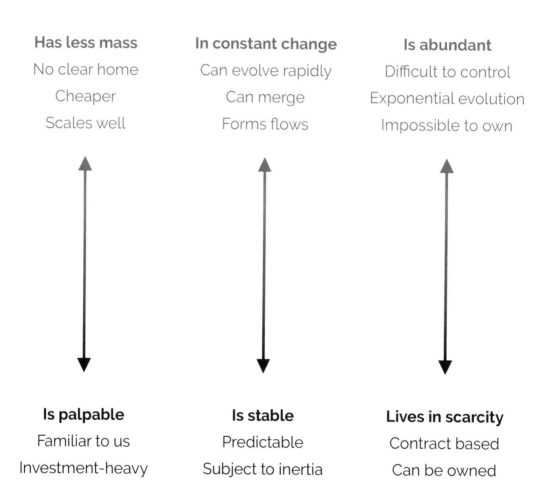

Has less mass
No clear home
Cheaper
Scales well

In constant change
Can evolve rapidly
Can merge
Forms flows

Is abundant
Difficult to control
Exponential evolution
Impossible to own

Is palpable
Familiar to us
Investment-heavy

Is stable
Predictable
Subject to inertia

Lives in scarcity
Contract based
Can be owned

More tangible

The old physical world we know so well.

the intangible relationships it fosters with its customers and other stakeholders. For instance, a brand's reputation, constructed digitally through customer reviews, social media interactions, and online engagements, will have a tangible impact on its market share and revenue.

The merger of the tangible and intangible in the digital space offers businesses unprecedented agility. Operations are no longer bound by physical constraints. Inventory management can leverage real-time data analytics, production lines can be optimized through digital simulations, and market strategies can be dynamically altered based on online consumer behavior. This agility allows businesses to respond to market changes with speed and precision, creating a competitive advantage.

The way businesses, stakeholders, and consumers perceive this intertwined realm plays a pivotal role in harnessing its potential. Recognizing the digital realm as a space that manifests both the tangible and intangible enables a more holistic approach to strategy formulation, risk assessment, and value creation.

The digital realm is a testament to the convergence of worlds, where tangible assets and intangible values coalesce. This new perspective necessitates a shift in operational strategies, business models, and value assessments, pushing businesses to innovate, adapt, and evolve in the face of a continually changing landscape.

EMBRACE THE FLOW

The convergence of these two worlds presents a paradigm where businesses can tap into the strengths of both, carving out competitive advantages.

Traditional asset valuations have often sidelined intangibles, focusing mainly on physical assets. However, in today's business landscape,

Characteristics of intangible elements

The intangible is not just about the absence of physical form; it's about the unique qualities that are embodied and harnessed to unlock unparalleled strategic advantages.

WEIGHTLESSNESS

Has less mass: Intangibles don't obey the laws of physics in the same way as tangibles.

No clear home: A belief or political ideology, for instance, can be held simultaneously in many places.

Economical and scalable: With little to no production cost, intangibles like software or knowledge can be distributed widely.

FLUIDITY

In constant change: Intangibles are dynamic. Think about the shift in social norms over the years.

Merging and flowing: When an idea merges with another, it forms a new thought stream, creating a flow of innovation and evolution.

Exponential evolution: As intangibles combine and recombine, their growth can often be exponential rather than linear.

ABUNDANCE

Limitless expansion: Unlike physical commodities, intangibles like digital twins or data can multiply and grow.

Elusive control: Digital entities, ideologies, and even trust are hard to control, making them incredibly challenging to own or restrain.

Unbounded growth: In a world without physical borders, the potential for expansion and influence is boundless.

Characteristics of tangible elements

The tangible realm pertains to the physical world. It's the realm of the concrete, the consistent, and the limited. For businesses, navigating the tangible is often about managing finite resources, dealing with physical constraints, and leveraging assets that have clear boundaries and definitions.

PALPABLE

Familiar to us: Tangible elements are those that we can directly perceive with our senses. They are concrete and identifiable, offering a sense of familiarity and comfort.

Investment-heavy: Tangible assets often require significant capital outlay. Whether it's machinery for a factory, real estate, or raw materials, tangible items often come with higher initial costs compared to intangibles.

STABLE

Predictable: Due to their physical nature, tangible elements usually operate within a predictable set of boundaries. For example, a machine can be expected to perform a specific task under given conditions.

Subject to inertia: Tangible elements resist sudden change. Just as it's hard to instantly stop a moving train, tangible assets can't always adapt or pivot rapidly in response to changing circumstances.

LIVES IN SCARCITY

Contract-based: Ownership and transactions related to tangible assets are typically governed by legal contracts.

Ownership: Unlike intangibles, where there can be ambiguity regarding ownership, tangible elements can be clearly owned, sold, or transferred. This provides a direct source of value, as ownership is recognized and can be legally enforced.

intangibles like innovation speed or data analysis capabilities often hold more value than physical infrastructure.

By straddling both the tangible and intangible realms, businesses can diversify their risk profiles. While tangible assets might be susceptible to physical damages or market fluctuations, intangibles offer a cushion. For instance, while a company's physical stores might suffer due to an unforeseen event, its customer loyalty or online services could still generate revenue.

The intangible realm is where innovation thrives. Concepts, ideas, and insights float freely, melding and morphing into groundbreaking solutions. By grounding these innovations in the tangible—translating novel ideas into physical products and services—companies can realize their potential and drive market disruption. Ironically, the flow of these intangible elements is often stifled within organizations by material-world concepts like control and ownership. This can materialize in the form of targets, metrics, and organizational silos. Typically, clients and partners are excluded from knowledge sharing and innovation processes, creating barriers to comprehensive innovation.

BALANCING POWERS

Both the tangible and intangible play crucial roles in engaging clients. While tangible products and services satisfy direct needs, intangibles like brand narratives, values, personal bonds, and corporate cultures foster deeper emotional connections. A strategy that celebrates both can foster stronger loyalty and trust.

In an era of rapid change, rigidity can be damaging. Companies that harness the intangible's fluid nature while grounding themselves in tangible realities can pivot more efficiently. This hybrid approach allows for dynamic business modeling, catering to evolving markets and consumer preferences. With technological advancements and shifting societal norms, the future leans toward the intangible. Companies that strategically integrate digital platforms, AI, data analytics, and other intangible assets into their operations will not only stay ahead of the curve but will future proof their businesses.

I bet you can't get that Madonna song out of your head now!

Immaterial spectrum

Elements that live in immaterial flows	Emotions
	Creativity
	Artificial intelligence
Elements designed to change flows	Knowledge
	Algorithms
Elements designed to create flows	Social media
	Data collection points
Intangible creations we see as more or less material	Webstores
Constructs designed to control material objects	Ownership
Constructs we perceive as tangible	Contracts
	Airplanes
Moving manmade objects	Buildings
Static manmade objects	Trees
Living natural objects	
Moving natural objects	Water
Static natural objects	Coal

An example of the Immaterial Spectrum. As we get closer to the top, personal preferences matter. So, feel free to create your own spectrum.

Playing around with the Immaterial Spectrum can help identify where your business operates.

Navigating the immaterial spectrum

Business thrives in the space between the two extremes of the fully material and the fully immaterial. Here can be found a spectrum of variety and possibility.

Consider, for instance, the wide range of materials we use for energy. At one end of the continuum is coal, a tangible resource that's been a staple for centuries. Its material characteristics are evident: it's palpable, solid to the touch, and clearly defined. The mining of coal is an investment-heavy venture, with machinery and manpower dedicated to its extraction. Its predictable nature, derived from centuries of use, makes it a stable source of energy. However, its tangible nature also means it's subject to scarcity—the coal we extract can't be replaced.

As we travel along the continuum toward the intangible, we encounter other resources. Oil, for example, introduces a level of intangibility when compared to coal. Its liquid state, extraction process, and the global politics surrounding it make it a more dynamic player in the energy game.

Gas pushes the boundaries even further. Its elusive nature, paired with its capability to be transported with lighter infrastructure, introduces greater intangibility. Yet, when we consider wind energy, the scales tip even further. The turbines are clearly tangible, but the wind they harness has more immaterial qualities than coal or gas. It's a force of nature, dynamic and ever-changing.

Solar energy, however, stands out as the epitome of the immaterial in the energy sector. While the solar panels themselves are tangible, the sunlight they harness is not. This energy source, abundant and available to all, requires the initial establishment of infrastructure and the mining of metals for panel production. Yet, once operational, solar panels consume significantly fewer finite resources than oil and gas, offering a more sustainable solution. Unlike coal production, there is no physical entity to be owned or sold in terms of the sunlight itself. Sunlight, in its ethereal form, is abundant, flowing freely and available for all to harness.

FASCINATION FOR ROCKS
IDEA OF A ROCK
STORY ABOUT A ROCK
CREATIVE IDEAS FOR ROCKS
KNOWLEDGE ABOUT ROCKS
BUSINESS PLAN FOR A ROCK COMPANY
ROCK BAND
DRAWING OF A ROCK
IMAGE OF A ROCK
A ROCK

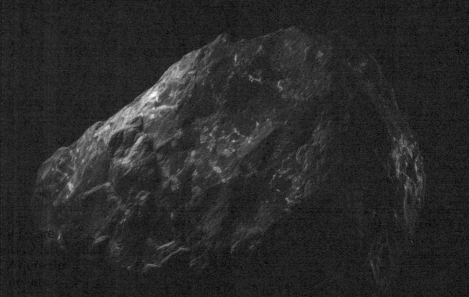

When we lay these energy sources along the immaterial spectrum, a fascinating picture emerges. Businesses that cling solely to the tangible may find themselves limited, bound by the confines of physical resources. Yet, those that embrace the intangible, recognizing its potential and pairing it with tangible assets, can unlock opportunities for unprecedented growth and innovation.

In essence, understanding the immaterial spectrum is not just about distinguishing between what's tangible and intangible. It's about recognizing the nuances, the gradations that exist between them. For businesses, this means identifying where their products, services, or resources lie on this spectrum, and how they can leverage the unique attributes of both the tangible and the intangible for success.

THE INTANGIBLE MASQUERADING AS THE TANGIBLE

While we can feel the weight of a book or touch the walls of a building, there are countless entities that, though immaterial, are perceived almost as if they were solid, tangible objects. Companies, contracts, patents, copyrights, religious institutions, nation states, money, and software fall into this nebulous category. These are among the many intangible constructs that have become deeply woven into the fabric of our societies.

At the heart of this phenomenon is the power of collective belief. Many of the intangibles we consider solid and real in the modern world are fundamentally rooted in shared convictions. Consider money: its value is not in the paper or metal, but in the collective trust that assigns it worth. Such entities serve as collective imaginaries—unspoken agreements based on shared understanding. When society believes in these constructs' legitimacy, they function effectively. The strength of this belief is evident in the repercussions that arise from breaking its associated conventions. Whether it's a breach of contract or a monetary fraud, violations against these intangible entities often lead to very tangible, sometimes severe, consequences in the physical realm.

Understanding the physical status of these immaterial constructs requires a historical perspective. Over time, the role of the intangible has evolved, reflecting the changing needs and complexities of human societies.

Early on, as societies began to form and grow in complexity, there was an

Elements that flow easily

Data   Ideas   Emotions

Talent

Creativity   Beliefs

Artificial intelligence   Thoughts

Brand   Knowledge   Hope

Metaverse   Trust   Attitudes

Intuition

Digital twins   Loyalty

Memories

Reputation

Software   Commitment   Wisdom

Political ideoligies   Spiritual convictions

Ideals   Faith

Social norms   Charisma

Companies   Friendship   Identity

Legacy

Copyrights   Morality

History   Cultural practices

Contracts   Patents   Religious doctrines   Values

Nation states

Laws   Customs

Elements that are more stable

Some elements are pliable and easy to merge. Others seem more solid and grounded. We can argue about the placement of each element, but it is important that we recognize that some elements thrive in a state of flow and others require support and consolidation. These are qualities that we should embrace.

imperative to introduce order and structure. Intangible mechanisms, from tribal affiliations to codified laws, emerged as tools of governance and control. These abstract constructs, such as kingdoms or religious doctrines, played an important role in organizing communities, defining hierarchies, and setting boundaries.

With the passage of time and the advent of revolutionary technologies, the intangible began to serve a different purpose: acceleration. Innovations, particularly in the realms of communication and information dissemination, meant that the world was now connected like never before. Immaterial tools and platforms became conduits for rapid exchange, learning, and collaboration.

What sets intangibles in motion?

To influence the immaterial, we must first comprehend its nature. Unlike the physical world, where force and matter interact, the immaterial world is shaped by elements like creativity, emotions, and beliefs. These elements are not static; they are dynamic and fluid, responding to various stimuli in unique ways. For instance, creativity is often sparked not by tangible rewards like a salary raise but by intangible boosts such as inspiration, knowledge, and a sense of purpose.

Just as physical energy moves material objects, intangible energy propels immaterial elements. To initiate movement in this realm, one must identify what amplifies these elements. Take againg creativity as an example—it flourishes under the influence of excitement, passion, and a conducive environment. In the workplace, rather than material incentives, people can be inspired by motivational speeches, learning from the success of others, and collaborating with diverse teams that provide access to a greater range of skills, capabilities, and experiences.

Some intangible elements possess an inherent fluidity, allowing them to merge and evolve with ease. This fluid nature can lead to a cascade of changes, creating a flow of ideas, a surge in data, or even sparking transformative eras

SELF-IMAGE
SENSE OF BELONGING
ADMIRATION
OPINIONS
TRENDS
BRAND
FAN
SMELL
WALKING
SNEAKERS

of innovation. During the digital age, this has been exemplified by phenomena like the viral spread of social media content or the explosive growth of online gaming communities where players create and share their worlds.

While focusing on the immaterial, it's vital to acknowledge its interconnectedness with the physical world. Physical events can profoundly impact the immaterial. Traumatic experiences like car accidents, for example, can leave lasting emotional scars. Similarly, in a business context, tangible actions and policies can significantly influence the intangible aspects of organizational culture, employee morale, and brand reputation.

AMPLIFICATION AND ATTRACTION

The amplification of one aspect of the immaterial can quickly result in the amplification of other aspects, creating a powerful and influential flow that can lead to growth, innovation, and transformation, impacting both individual and collective experiences. It's a subtle art that combines understanding human psychology, social dynamics, and the power of ideas to create a lasting impact. This phenomenon is evident in the world of startups, where an innovative idea, when amplified by enthusiasm and strategic networking, can attract investors, customers, and media attention, resulting in exponential growth.

Amplification in the immaterial world involves enhancing the presence, impact, or effect of an intangible element, making it more powerful or influential. This process "turns up the volume," intensifying ideas, emotions, and values.

Consider the concept of Sisu, a Finnish term for extraordinary determination in the face of adversity. Amplifying this trait within a community can be achieved through storytelling, celebrating examples of resilience, and creating support structures that encourage this gritty mindset.

The dynamics of amplification and attraction in social media—and increasingly in traditional media, too—are key in determining which platforms thrive and which decline. Successful platforms are those that continuously amplify elements that enhance user experience and engagement, leveraging these improvements to attract more users, content creators, and commercial partnerships. The flow effect causes only a handful of services to dominate at a time.

Is that the French football player?

PROVOCATION:
CORPORATE GLUE

URS MERKEL

Urs is passionate about data science and the psychology of organizational behavior. He is the founder of soft.fact and serves as the company's Chief Vision Officer. Urs also hosts the podcast teamfrequenz, which focuses on the psychometrics of team dynamics.

Corporate culture is one of the biggest sources of competitive advantage. Leaders know this. For some time, companies have tried to understand and capture the allusive immaterial elements of a culture. Understanding behavioral patterns in predicting human behavior and reciprocal relationships separate excellent companies from the mediocre. The challenge lies in making culture and behavioral patterns visible, so we can understand the needs of people and respond to them.

Many organizations understand the benefits but face a challenge in utilizing intangible psychological traits. These are rooted in personality, sociological role tendencies, communication patterns, and motives, among other factors. As a data scientist and organizational behavior psychologist, I refer to them as "soft facts." They begin as formless and intangible, yet through measurement, they become something we can interpret, discuss, and develop. They gain form and their connections become apparent.

Excellent managers have a gut feeling for handling these aspects of work. They put in the effort to learn how to handle soft facts. These managers seek to create an environment beneficial to human wellbeing and relationships.

Many organizations understand and value soft facts as the immaterial glue in keeping their people together, healthy, and productive. This is what their managers are expected to deliver.

MAKING CULTURAL FLOWS TANGIBLE

When the intangible becomes measurable and "more tangible," it becomes easier for people, either alone or collectively, to reflect on and work toward needs-oriented collaboration and human-centered organizational design.

For many companies, this enables a huge evolution in the work environment. Work can be illustrated as a triangle, encompassing expertise, methodology, and the human-centric. In many cases, this triangle is still biased toward the first two. But understanding and utilizing psychometrics forces the triad into a balance.

By providing understandable insights into our own psychological and sociological behavior, the whole concept of self-reflection and acting on what we discover into action becomes a data-driven measurable discipline.

Now individuals, teams, and leaders can use validated data points to track growth and work on improving relationships. Company culture and team dynamics become more predictable.

Applying psychometrics makes it possible to explain who brings which communication patterns to a group, and to identify the values and intrinsic motives that influence decision-making. It also helps us understand who gets the most energy from taking on certain sociological roles in a group. This has a far greater impact on leadership styles and their contextual relevance than anything that can be learned in a classroom.People become aware of their individual traits and how they affect their behavior and interactions.

Validated information helps foster healthy relationships, raising awareness of mutual needs, behavioral tendencies, and concern for an environment in which they can flourish for the good of the community. Different layers of a community become visible and can be sliced and diced like a Rubik's cube.

What sounds like a challenge is, thanks to the data-driven approach, merely a task that needs to be executed. Nevertheless, this requires awareness and consistency to achieve behavioral improvement, benefiting how people interact, collaborate, and work.

WITH GREAT POWER COMES GREAT RESPONSIBILITY

Making the intangible visible poses certain dangers. One involves manipulation, controlling other people's behavior. Another centers on self-growth.

As responsible leaders, we need to be aware of both, operating transparently and building a culture of trust. There is no right or wrong, only differences which can benefit us all.

Quirks of
the immaterial

Immaterial elements have some special qualities that differentiate them from their material counterparts. These differences create interesting dynamics that can be used in business. For example, how we perceive ownership, how scarcity can find new forms, or how branding plays various roles.

OWNERSHIP AND SENSE OF OWNERSHIP

The term ownership refers to a legal right or possession of something, whether tangible like property or intangible like intellectual rights. It's a clear-cut, formal relationship backed by law, granting specific rights and duties.

In contrast, a sense of ownership is the emotional and psychological connection one feels toward a possession, task, role, project, or opinion. It's not about legal entitlement but about personal investment and responsibility. While legal ownership offers concrete rights, a sense of ownership infuses passion and commitment, driving individuals to treat matters with genuine care, regardless of legal ties. Understanding this distinction is vital, especially in contexts where nurturing a sense of ownership can amplify results, even without formal ownership in play.

This feeling, which goes beyond legal rights and enters the realm of emotional investment, can profoundly influence various facets of a business.

An employee who feels a sense of ownership over their work or project is more motivated to see it succeed. This goes beyond mere task completion; it's about seeing the bigger picture, understanding the importance of one's role in the larger organizational context, and proactively working toward the company's objectives.

When clients feel a sense of ownership over a product or service, it means they're emotionally invested. This deepens the relationship between the client and the company, as the client sees themselves as part of the journey, not just a recipient of a product. A client's sense of ownership often translates to loyalty. They become advocates and champions for the brand, ensuring repeat business and word-of-mouth referrals.

In successful partnerships, if both parties feel a shared sense of ownership over the combined mission or project, they're more likely to invest time, resources, and energy to ensure its success.

Partnerships anchored in a sense of ownership are more sustainable, focused on long-term growth. Both parties are invested in not just immediate returns, but the broader vision and potential of their joint venture.

The sense of ownership, while intangible, wields significant influence over the dynamics of a business. By fostering this feeling among employees, clients, and partners, businesses can build a foundation of trust, loyalty, and mutual growth.

While the concepts of ownership and sense of ownership have much in common, they are by nature very different. They are both intangible, but ownership is rooted in the physical realm. Its effects are profoundly tangible, tethering rights to finite objects and resources.

Sense of ownership is fluid, deeply personal, and intangible in its purest form. Unlike ownership, a sense of ownership is nebulous, constantly evolving, and challenging to pin down. Its beauty lies in its abundance. While an asset can have a single owner, a multitude can harbor a shared sense of ownership toward it. With community projects, cultural heritage, and favorite sports teams, this shared sentiment can knit individuals together, fueling collective passion, responsibility, and pride.

Businesses that can balance and harness both realms will not only recognize the full potential of their assets but also craft strategies that resonate in a multifaceted business ecosystem. For the modern executive, appreciating both the seen and the unseen isn't just a philosophical pursuit, but a business imperative.

ARTIFICIAL SCARCITY

In the realm of the tangible, scarcity is an inherent quality. Diamonds are prized not just for their shimmering beauty, but for their rarity. An original artwork carries not only the artist's vision but also the distinction of being unique. Yet, as we delve deeper into the digital era, we find the concept of scarcity manipulated, stretched, and redefined.

Historically, scarcity was a result of natural limitations. Resources such as water, minerals, or land are finite. As such, their availability has always been restricted. Similarly, a handcrafted piece of design is valued because of the labor, skill, and singular vision required to create it. However, the digital world defies these limitations. Here, duplication is not just possible, but it's often instantaneous and cost-free. One might wonder then, how can anything digital ever be scarce?

Yet, recognizing the value of rarity, companies have introduced artificial scarcity into the digital realm. This is done not because of any inherent limitation but rather as a strategic maneuver. Online events might limit slots to give a feeling of exclusivity, or prestigious platforms might become invite-only to drive up their perceived value. Digital currencies put caps on their mining, and unique non-fungible tokens are sold for exorbitant prices, both tapping into the same human desire for rarity.

The underlying reasons for creating this scarcity where none exists naturally are multifaceted. Limiting access or availability makes a product or service more desirable, allowing sellers to command higher prices. Additionally, the fear of missing out (FOMO) has become a potent tool in the marketer's arsenal. By hinting at a limited window of opportunity, providers can instigate a rush among consumers eager not to miss out. Moreover, in a world inundated with free digital content, creators often face challenges with monetization. Introducing artificial scarcity provides a strategy for converting digital assets into tangible monetary gains.

As the digital domain continues to evolve, it's fascinating to observe how it blurs the lines between the real and the virtual. This artificial scarcity can seem contrived, but it taps into very real human emotions and behaviors. The value of a digitally scarce item isn't in its bits and bytes, but in the human desire for distinction, belonging, and ownership. As we move forward, the interplay between scarcity and abundance will undoubtedly challenge our perceptions of value and worth in our increasingly virtual existence.

BRANDS CAN NAVIGATE IN BOTH WORLDS

The concept of a brand remains elusive, lacking a universally accepted definition. It's a flexible idea, perceived differently by various people. For some, it's merely the logo on a sneaker, a simple visual identifier. For others, it's a multifunctional marketing tool, adaptable and versatile in its use. There are those who view it as a sacred entity, transcending the company it represents, embodying a promise, a story, an image, a feeling, a sense of unity, and a vision of a better future. This great versatility and elusiveness is because a brand is doubly immaterial: an intangible representation of company, which itself is an intangible entity.

A brand can be both tangible and intangible, with its fluidity making it a highly adaptable tool. On one hand, a brand can be seen as an immaterial replication of a product, an intangible illusion that holds value even without a tangible offering. The notion that "Your brand is what people say about you when you are not in the room" points to how value creation can be based solely on perception. On the other hand, a brand is a means to control intangibles. By actively cultivating their brand, companies can attract desired attributes and attach them to their brand, essentially bottling specific emotions and associating them with their products and services.

Brand can play multiple roles. As a resource, a brand's value can be calculated, treated as a company asset, and, to some extent, owned. It can be restricted and controlled, shaping how it's used and perceived. Additionally, a brand is integral to company processes, aiding in the development of a unified internal culture, attracting partners, and serving as a dynamic tool for marketing and communication. Branding plays a crucial role in shaping a company's sustainability, safety, and quality culture by setting standards and goals.

As part of a company's offering, a strong brand can differentiate it from its competitors. People are naturally drawn to brands that appeal to them and may avoid others, regardless of the similarity in offerings. Because of its immaterial nature, a brand can forge strong connection with clients' emotions. People may develop a sense of ownership over certain brands, incorporating them into their personal narratives. In this way, brands transcend their commercial origin, becoming part of individual identities and stories.

Case against money

In business books, money has long stood as a tangible representation of value, bridging the gap between physical assets and perceived worth. But with the shift from the tangible to the intangible, a traditional understanding of money seems increasingly archaic and limiting, making it an obsolete measure that prevents companies from fully capitalizing on the vast potential of the intangible realm.

Historically, money arose as a solution to the barter system's inefficiencies. Coins, notes, and eventually digital figures provided a tangible metric to assign value to goods and services. Over time, businesses, economies, and societies were constructed around this monolithic metric, making money the cornerstone of value exchange.

THE SHIFT FROM SCARCITY TO ABUNDANCE

The tangible world operates on principles of scarcity: limited resources, finite real estate, and physical constraints. In this environment, money helped quantify value where scarcity was the rule. However, the intangible world operates on abundance. Digital assets, intellectual property, online communities, and virtual realities aren't bound by traditional constraints. In such an environment, the finite metric of money struggles to encapsulate the infinite potential and value of intangible assets.

Consider the realm of social media. Platforms like X or Instagram harness user-generated content, community engagement, and network effects. While they generate revenue, the true value of these platforms lies in data, influence, connectivity, and community. These are intangibles that money can't adequately measure. By focusing solely on monetary metrics, businesses risk underestimating or overlooking the multidimensional value of intangible assets.

While money offers a standardized metric, it also acts as a tether, binding businesses to traditional valuation models. Companies entrenched in these models often find it challenging to innovate, diversify revenue streams, or fully harness the intangible realm's potential. They become risk-averse, focusing on immediate monetary returns rather than the long-term, expansive potential of intangible assets.

TOWARD NEW METRICS OF VALUE

For businesses to thrive in a world dominated by intangibles, there's a pressing need for new value metrics. Consider the rise of cryptocurrencies, DAOs, and decentralized finance (DeFi) platforms. They challenge traditional monetary systems, introducing fluidity, decentralization, and new valuation paradigms. Similarly, metrics related to user engagement, data capitalization, and brand sentiment are emerging as indicators of value in the intangible space.

While money has been a steadfast metric for millennia, the dawn of the intangible era necessitates a reevaluation of its role. It's not about completely discarding money but recognizing its limitations in a rapidly evolving landscape. Businesses, to remain agile and forward-thinking, must transcend traditional monetary metrics and embrace a more holistic understanding of value that resonates with the boundless potential of the intangible world.

This could even be the end of companies as we know them. Maybe the questions are as simple as this: Do we want to focus on creating money or on creating value? If the latter, what is the best method of organization that will enable us to accomplish it?

PROVOCATION:
THE FUTURE OF MONEY
THE ADVENT OF A HELIOGENIC CIVILIZATION

THOMAS SCHINDLER

Thomas has a background in technology, environmental sustainability, and community engagement, which he leverages to address some of the most pressing challenges of our time and create a good world. He is the co-founder of the custom software development firm DELODI, and has been instrumental in the leadership of the multidisciplinary Project MIRACLE, the Initiative for the Regenerative Market-Economy (IRM), the Global Impact Tech Alliance (GITA), and MOTHERLAND, which bridges between African startups and farmers.

IN Superintelligence, Nick Bostrom presents "the paperclip maximiser" thought experiment, underscoring the critical need for well-defined AI goals. He posits that an AI with a simple aim, such as creating a million paper clips, could inadvertently consume our planet in pursuit of increasingly perfect production.

For two centuries, we've been part of an analogous AI experiment, not powered by silicon but by our brains' organic computation. Steered by an "invisible hand,'" the market these brains have created excels at converting nature to waste, precipitating various interlinked crises. Perhaps this "hand" is more akin to a less favorable body part.

Money, the market's information system, serves as a guide. Its design crucially influences market behavior. Currently, money creation is exponential, with money supply (M3) doubling every decade. To maintain purchasing power, we need an equivalent value store backing our currency. Since 1971, this has been our productivity, quantified by gross domestic product (GDP).

GDP, too, doubles approximately every twenty years. Essentially, it gauges the volume of atoms moved in a region over time. Since moving atoms necessitates energy, it's unsurprising that energy consumption, closely tied to GDP, also doubles every three decades.

This system operates on a 19-terawatt continuous energy supply, predominantly sourced from fossil fuels. The depletion of these fuels and the resulting negative impact on our planet's chemistry threaten our living conditions. Efforts to shift to an electric-powered economy often ignore the biophysical reality of limited material access at our current level of innovation.

Attempting to innovate out of this predicament is like boarding a plane with a 50/50 crash risk, hopeful that the pilot will fix the issue mid-flight. Even if successful, this approach aggravates the planet's heat issue for future generations. Utilizing abundant fusion or geothermal energy will generate unabsorbable waste heat. Future generations may need to construct infrastructure specifically to expel this excess heat that has been trapped on Earth. The physics are non-negotiable.

"ATTEMPTING TO INNOVATE OUT OF THIS PREDICAMENT IS LIKE BOARDING A PLANE WITH A 50/50 CRASH RISK, HOPEFUL THAT THE PILOT WILL FIX THE ISSUE MID-FLIGHT."

Our current monetary system is self-consuming. However, as with many transitions, we face a choice: react in fear or embrace opportunity and growth. Opting for growth hints at a vast economy harmonious with nature's principles, contrasting starkly with present practices.

At present, humans and nature serve a system that disregards their longevity and wellbeing. Imagine reversing this, placing life center stage, at the heart of all activities. Life fosters more life, enhancing conditions for its own proliferation. We are integral to life and so are our descendants.

Over many billions of years, life has orchestrated a vast circular economy known as nature. This process relies on six atoms—Carbon, Hydrogen, Oxygen, Nitrogen, Phosphorus, and Sulfur—to forge all conceivable forms of life on Earth. As with the economy, this natural system also demands energy, harnessing the 172,000 terawatts of energy beamed by the sun, that colossal fusion reactor in the sky.

This is freely available bounty. Just like the web standards created by Tim Berners-Lee and the UNIX operating systems developed by Ken Thompson,

Dennis Ritchie, and their colleagues at Bell Labs—contributions that form a significant part of the internet infrastructure that contributes 15% of global GDP today.

What if there were an open, free foundation for a materials-based economy, aligned with nature's principles? An economy dependent on the immense pool of raw resources, including atoms and energy, could dwarf today's by three orders of magnitude, rendering the current economic model obsolete. All the while, it would harmonize with life's rhythms. To some, this might seem fantastical, yet it's already unfolding in global science labs and through innovative business ventures.

Picture a world where every individual possesses equal, free access to all materials needed for a fulfilling life. In this scenario, people and communities would have greatly enhanced control over their life circumstances, coupled with significantly increased opportunities to contribute to mutual flourishing. Such a shift could profoundly alter how money functions, signaling the advent of a heliogenic civilization.

"AS WE FIND OURSELVES AT A PIVOTAL MOMENT IN HISTORY, THE ADVENT OF HELIOGENIC TECHNOLOGIES MAKES A MATERIALLY ABUNDANT EXCHANGE SYSTEM NOT JUST VIABLE BUT ESSENTIAL."

Two decades ago, Bernard Lietaer, who had recently overseen the introduction of the Euro and previously directed the Central Bank of Belgium, mentored me on the intricacies of currency systems. He often recounted a story about Ghent, a city grappling with intractable issues relating to illegal immigration, substance abuse, violence, and a pervasive sense of desolation.

Bernard engaged with the local community, inquiring about their desires. Many expressed a longing for land to cultivate food and flowers, a space for regeneration. Responding, he facilitated the use of an unused plot for such purposes, introducing a unique currency system. This currency could be earned through community-enhancing activities: acts of kindness, street cleaning, beautifying windows with flowers, and house painting.

Remarkably, both environment and inhabitants swiftly transformed.

Inspired by this success, Bernard conceived a grand vision, one that took me years to fully comprehend and only became clear within the framework of the heliogenic civilization. He wanted to create a central bank of dreams.

Under Bernard's worldwide scheme, every individual could declare their dream to back their unique currency. As others contributed to realizing someone's dream, that individual could generate new currency. In a world with 10 billion distinct currencies, everyday transactions like buying bread would be challenging, but that's precisely the intent. The gift economy endures.

In fact, our private economic behavior often relegates financial capital to the background. Our engagements are primarily with social, cultural, experiential, intellectual, material, living, and spiritual capital. Intriguingly, these aren't commodities traded for money; they circulate as gifts, in a perpetual cycle of community and generosity.

As we find ourselves at a pivotal moment in history, the advent of heliogenic technologies makes a materially abundant exchange system not just viable but essential. This leap is not merely practical; it's a critical reorientation from the myopic pursuit of growth to a more enlightened symbiosis with life's rhythms. In contrast to the 'paperclip maximizer' scenario, where AI's blind ambition could devour our world, we're consciously steering towards a more integrated existence.

Imagine a future where our economic pulse aligns not with the sterile ticking of GDP, but with the vibrant heartbeat of life itself. This heliogenic civilization shifts us from being mere components in a vast machine to active participants in a system where every action reverberates with purpose. Here, the value of currency transcends its buying power to embody dreams actualized, communities forged, and ecosystems regenerated.

This shift transcends technological innovation; it's a recalibration of our cultural and intellectual compass. It invites a redefinition of success, not as a solitary climb but as a collective journey towards holistic wellbeing. It's an invitation to reposition ourselves in the universe, not as dominators but as co-creators, in a complex, interwoven narrative of existence.

If you quietly listen to your heart's response, you will realize that it already knows these weird words to be true.

THE TOOLS

How do we navigate the expanding mesh of tangibles and intangibles? How do we include them both in our business strategy so that they make sense?

Introduction to
IMMATERIAL MAP

"Beyond the ink and parchment, lies a world uncharted by the physical eye, but navigable by the visionary mind."

THIS TOOLSET:

- Provides a platform for discovery.
- Helps simplify our offering and our story.
- Finds synergies between business units and partners.
- Serves as a foundation for our strategy work.

- Assists us in evaluating our existing strategy.
- Enables us to analyze competitor's strategies.
- Is a facilitation tool for consultants and managers
- Creates a common language for the future.

I did not want to create an Immaterial Canvas. Instead, I made an Immaterial Map. There is a huge difference. At best, a canvas can help us have well-structured discussions as we complete it. But it has a rigid structure because of its predefined segments. The content may differ, but the structure is always the same.

A map, by contrast, begins as a white and empty space. The more you discover more, the more patterns being to emerge. These patterns form different journeys and stories. Maps are great tools for visualizing the landscape of a particular domain, such as a market, industry, or technology. They help us understand positioning, movement, and evolution. They are more organic, allowing flows and patterns to emerge.

I find a map to be more demanding than a canvas. We may feel a sense of accomplishment when we fill in a canvas, ticking the relevant boxes, but a map requires more of us, providing fewer guard rails. That's why I created a map: To bug you!

These tools are not magic. They stretch us, they require effort, they make us think. We have to be innovative and creative. We need to see patterns where others see emptiness. We need to step out of our comfort zones and be courageous and experimental. When working with others, we also must be open and supportive. New ideas are fragile and quickly turn to dust when trampled on.

For those willing to invest the time, this map can yield interesting, even groundbreaking findings. It can challenge us to look at the world around us with fresh eyes, and it points the way to deeper and more involved discussion with colleagues and stakeholders.

The basic layout of the map is very simple. A rectangle. (I have rounded the two top corners to illustrate the immaterial nature of the "the North". And because nobody will pay for a rectangle, but rounded corners make it something worth buying.)

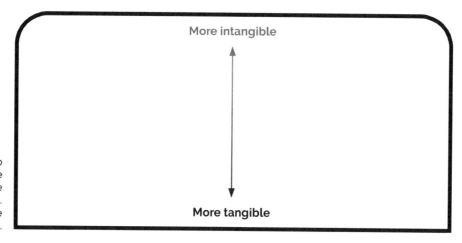

The higher we go on the map the more intangible elements are. The bottom is the tangible area.

"New things need to fit old boxes."
To introduce new ways of thinking we should always link it back to what we already know. This is why the map is sliced into traditional business segments. We have Resources, Processes, Offering and Client Needs.

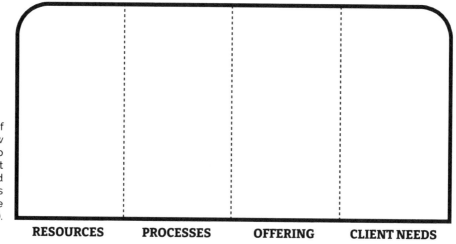

You may of course draw your own map and folds (but remember to add rounded corners to add some class to it).

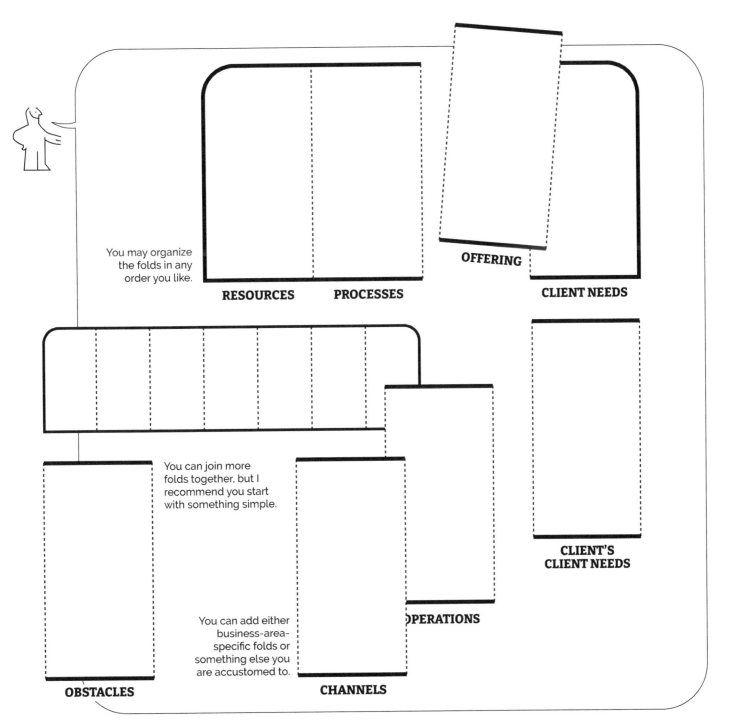

You may organize the folds in any order you like.

RESOURCES　　**PROCESSES**

OFFERING

CLIENT NEEDS

You can join more folds together, but I recommend you start with something simple.

You can add either business-area-specific folds or something else you are accustomed to.

OBSTACLES

CHANNELS

OPERATIONS

CLIENT'S CLIENT NEEDS

LET'S START WITH A STORY

EXPLAIN YOUR BUSINESS

Tell it as a simple story and write it down.

Example 1:
"We are a technically advanced partner providing equipment for heavy industry. We are specialized in supporting global mining companies."

Example 2:
"We import lash extension kits. Our clients are both beauty studios and private people. Our main sales channel is our strong community that organizes trainings and events."

Example 3:
"We are an office furniture producer and office interior design consulting company. Our people are well attuned to the trends of office design. We have a very deep relationship with our clients, and they trust us in all interior-design-related projects."

SUPPORTING QUESTIONS:

Who do you serve?
How do you help them?

What is your offering?
What problem do you solve?

What are your key resources?
What extraordinary things
do you have?

What is your
process like?

Why do your clients use
your products/services?
What are their needs?

How do you do it?

STRATEGY JOURNEY

1

LET'S START
WITH A STORY

Tell it as a simple story
and write it down.

2

PUT YOUR STORY
ON THE MAP

Separate components
and place them on
the map.

3

MOVE THE PIECES
AROUND

Assess their place
on the immaterial
spectrum.

4

UNBUNDLE
ELEMENTS

Break them down to
be free to move on
the map.

6

ANALYZE AND
DEVELOP

5

EXPLAIN IT AS A STORY AGAIN

To check if it has changed or if it
makes sense.

H

IMMATERIAL
RESOURCES

F

IMMATERIAL
PROCESSES

D

IMMATERIAL
OFFERING

B

CLIENT'S
IMMATERIAL
NEEDS

G

MATERIAL
RESOURCES

E

MATERIAL
PROCESSES

C

MATERIAL
OFFERING

A

CLIENT'S
MATERIAL
NEEDS

PLACE THE ELEMENTS ON THE MAP

Break your story down to components: Resources, Processes, Offering, Needs. You can fill the obvious gaps.
Don't worry how it looks or if some parts are still empty. This is the starting point.

Example story:
"We are a technically advanced partner providing equipment for heavy industry. We are specialized in supporting global mining companies."

This becomes...

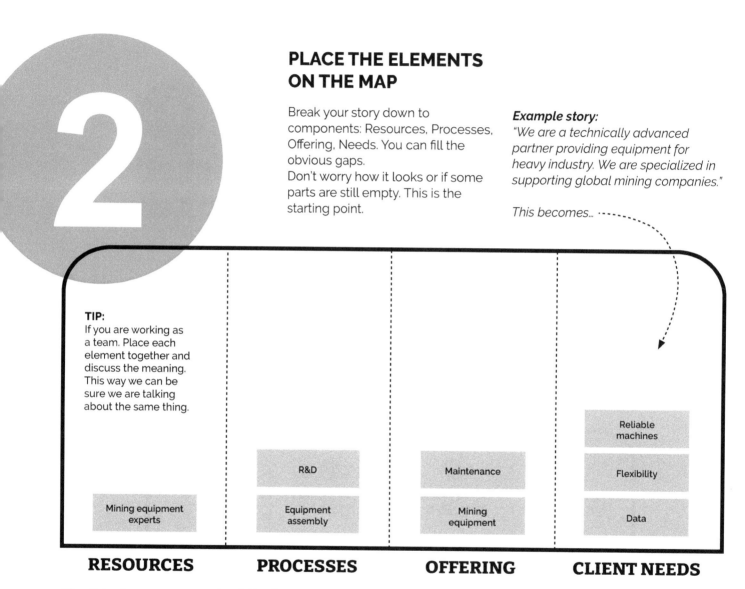

TIP:
If you are working as a team. Place each element together and discuss the meaning. This way we can be sure we are talking about the same thing.

R&D

Mining equipment experts

Equipment assembly

Maintenance

Mining equipment

Reliable machines

Flexibility

Data

RESOURCES   **PROCESSES**   **OFFERING**   **CLIENT NEEDS**

After this phase, your map should look something like this.

MOVE THE ELEMENTS UP AND DOWN

Estimate their level of intangibility. Push them up if they are more intangible and down if they are more tangible.

There are no absolutes here. It is all relative. Things are more intangible or tangible than others. If you are doing this as a team, there are likely to be lengthy and engaging discussions as you try to grasp the concepts and come to some kind of agreement. Take your time.

HELPFUL QUESTIONS:

Is it physical? Can you pinpoint its location? If YES, it is probably more on the material side.

Can someone see it? Does it have a big mass? Is it easy to control or own? Can you measure it precisely? If NO, it should be placed somewhere in the upper part of the map.

There is an additional guide on page 115. At this point you will probably come up with plenty of new elements to put on the map. Feel free to do so but be mindful not to clog up the whole map.

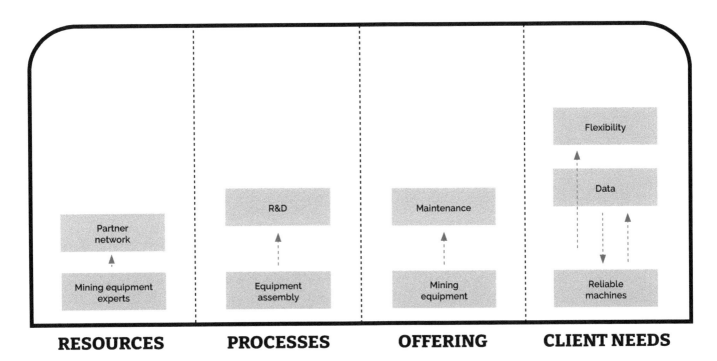

RESOURCES   **PROCESSES**   **OFFERING**   **CLIENT NEEDS**

TIP:
You can start working on the map from either end.
Do what feels easier or more relevant to your business.

UNBUNDLE

Some things are absolutely impossible to place on the map because they are both tangible and intangible or because the intangible is nested within the tangible. In these cases, they should be unbundled.

Business area expert, for example, should be unbundled into expert (human) and business area expertise (their knowledge and experience). This might feel counterintuitive as, at first glance, the expertise is associated with the expert. But unbundling comes in handy when we try to find motivating factors for resources or seek to identify new resources.

Your client might ask you for data when their real need is for knowledge.

TIP:
To avoid fistfights, it can be useful to have discussion about how each team member interprets each word. That helps establish shared understanding.

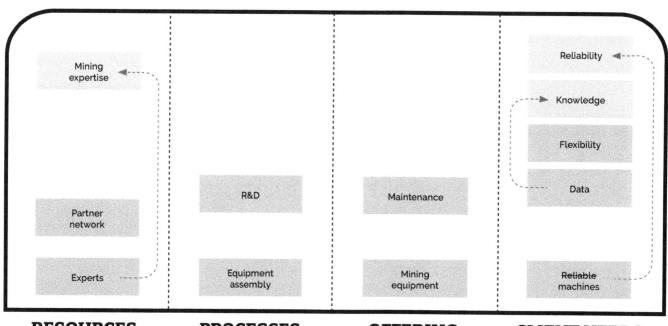

RESOURCES   **PROCESSES**   **OFFERING**   **CLIENT NEEDS**

This phase can be a bit messy. You might have only a few items or way too many. But don't panic!

TELL YOUR STORY AGAIN

Has the narrative changed?
Why? Why not?

Tell the story once in a while during this process. The aim is to keep it simple and make it easy to explain.

The A.C.M.E. Method

To aid your journey across the strategy map, you can employ the A.C.M.E. method.

Add: Introduce new elements that seem relevant and promising. These could be new services, products, or partnerships.

Connect: Look for potential connections between different elements on your map. These connections can spark new discussions and ideas, leading to innovative solutions.

Modify: Adapt existing elements. This could involve tweaking your services, altering your marketing approach, or changing internal processes to increase efficiency.

Erase: Sometimes, removing an element is as crucial as adding one. Identify aspects that hinder cohesion or don't align with your strategic vision and consider eliminating them.

THE ART OF PLAYFUL STRATEGY MAPPING

Now that you have roughly outlined your current strategy, the next phase of the journey is all about exploration and innovation. It's where the hard work begins, but it's also where the most exciting opportunities for growth and differentiation emerge.

Your Immaterial Map is not just a tool, it's a playground for ideas. The key here is to play across the map, exploring every corner without getting hung up on details. Great ideas are often delicate in their infancy. They need space to breathe and evolve.

Remember, on this map, there is no hierarchy of direction. Up is not better than down. The goal is to find a strategy that works for you, setting you apart from your competitors. This is not about following a predetermined path but about carving your own.

A critical aspect of your strategy will involve making informed choices about the various parts of your Immaterial Map. Each section plays a different role in your overarching strategy.

This chapter is not intended simply as a guide but as an invitation to experiment. Embrace innovation, play with ideas, and be open to unorthodox approaches. This journey is about discovering a strategy that resonates deeply with your unique vision and the distinct needs of your clients. It's a process of continuous learning, adaptation, and growth.

As you delve into the next phases, let your creativity flow, and allow your Immaterial Map to be a living, evolving representation of your vision. Remember, the most successful strategies often emerge from the most unexpected places.

Happy exploring!

HELPFUL QUESTIONS FOR THE EXPLORERS

As you dive into more detail, break apart existing elements, and bring in new ones, we are faced with plenty of questions and choices.

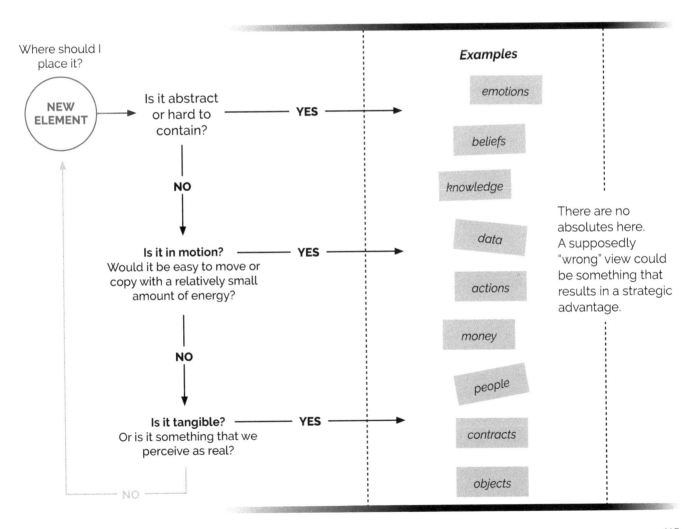

Where should I place it?

NEW ELEMENT

Is it abstract or hard to contain? — YES →

NO ↓

Is it in motion?
Would it be easy to move or copy with a relatively small amount of energy? — YES →

NO ↓

Is it tangible?
Or is it something that we perceive as real? — YES →

NO

Examples

emotions

beliefs

knowledge

data

actions

money

people

contracts

objects

There are no absolutes here. A supposedly "wrong" view could be something that results in a strategic advantage.

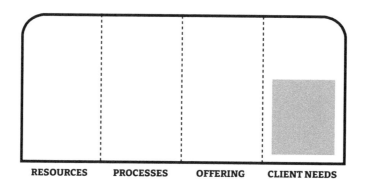

RESOURCES PROCESSES OFFERING CLIENT NEEDS

CLIENT'S "REAL" NEEDS

Tangible needs relate to clients' specific, concrete requirements—what they can touch, measure, and evaluate. These are the physical products, services, and outcomes that fulfill a direct purpose or function. Understanding and delivering tangible needs is essential for immediate client satisfaction and forms the foundation of a business's value proposition.

Listing tangible needs should be straightforward for business professionals, as these are the clear-cut demands that inform a client's purchasing decisions. They are rooted in practicality and necessity, allowing for a direct and objective approach to problem-solving and value delivery.

HELPFUL QUESTIONS

What are they paying us for?

What is the tangible outcome we enable?

What needs lie behind the obvious one? (Does the customer want hiking boots, dry feet, or better hiking trips?)

1. **Start with the obvious.**

   Aim to identify your client's most concrete needs and how they relate to what you offer. You should be looking for an object, action, or outcome.

2. Acknowledge that along with tangible needs, a client may also possess intangible needs that often complement the tangible ones. For example, "I want a car that earns my colleagues' respect."

3. Sometimes, a tangible need is satisfied by addressing an intangible one. For instance, a company might seek to acquire more knowledge and talent (intangible need) to develop new revenue streams (tangible need).

4. Are people looking for a shortcut? It may be that your client wants to identify time savings to progress more rapidly or accelerate a process. Please refer to the tool on page 119.

6 A

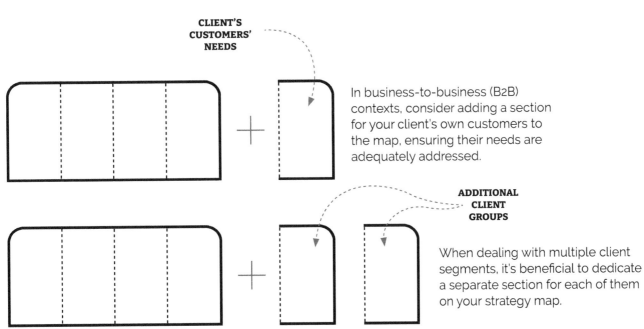

CLIENT'S CUSTOMERS' NEEDS

In business-to-business (B2B) contexts, consider adding a section for your client's own customers to the map, ensuring their needs are adequately addressed.

ADDITIONAL CLIENT GROUPS

When dealing with multiple client segments, it's beneficial to dedicate a separate section for each of them on your strategy map.

WHY IS THIS IMPORTANT?

When a client exclaims "That is exactly what I need!" it is a clear indicator of success. If you find it challenging to pinpoint your client's material needs, it is likely that you are complicating your client's decision-making process. This is especially critical in B2B transactions, where decisions are often collective and influenced by objective, tangible metrics rather than emotional judgment. Those involved are typically assessed based on quantifiable results.

If you wish to address a bigger purpose or focus on sustainability, it is advisable to add a fold for "the world" or "planet."

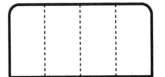

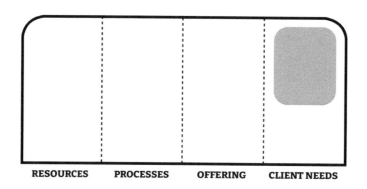

RESOURCES   PROCESSES   OFFERING   CLIENT NEEDS

IMMATERIAL NEEDS

While many believe that logic and rationality dominate their personal decision-making process, multiple studies have shown that emotional and other intangible factors play a critical role. This dichotomy is crucial in understanding client behavior and tailoring offerings to meet both their tangible and intangible needs.

Marketing books are filled with intangible needs, from identifying purpose to achieving self-actualization, from the social to the purely selfish.

In a B2B context, it is helpful to approach this from both a personal and organizational angle. What does the company want and what do the people working there want? What are the extrinsic and intrinsic needs?

Extrinsic needs are driven by external rewards and recognitions. For a business, these could manifest as a desire for market dominance or brand recognition.

Conversely, intrinsic needs are internally motivated both for individuals (personal values, intellectual challenge, creative expression) and organizations (innovation, ethical standards, corporate culture).

1. **List all possible immaterial needs.**

   First you can paint with broader strokes and have an open mind. What do they want to feel? How do they want to perceive themselves? What do they want to learn? What do they want to create? What really drives them?

2. Narrow the list down to what is truly relevant and try to organize them in order of intangibility.

3. Discuss how these elements are connected to material needs.

4. Explore how these elements can be used as resources.

> **BREATH**
>
> It is okay not to know. If you cannot identify your client's immaterial needs yet, leave this section blank. Better that than a page filled with invented garbage. The needs will emerge in due course.

INTANGIBLE VALUE LADDER

EXTRA

③ Intangible value

How do you do it?

What intangible value do you provide?

Examples: pride, sense of belonging, sense of ownership, sense of achievement, sense of superiority, hope, loyalty, trust, spirituality...

② Time

Do you help your clients save time?

☐ Yes

☐ No

How do you do it?

① Basic needs

Are you providing some of these?

☐ Shelter ☐ Vital medication ☐ Physical safety ☐ Basic nutrition

☐ No

This tool challenges you to examine your value proposition. Maybe the only thing you are selling is time? If your offering does not directly address basic needs, it is likely to be focused on a shortcut—a means to save time or to enhance life in some way. If not that, then you are providing intangible value. Your product or service is merely a vehicle for delivering that intangible value.

119

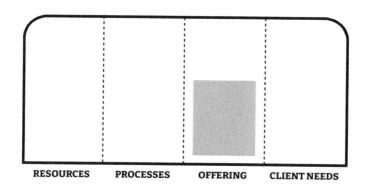

RESOURCES   PROCESSES   OFFERING   CLIENT NEEDS

MATERIAL OFFERING

Material offerings are tangible products or services packaged in a way that they are perceived as physical items. Their primary advantage lies in their straightforward nature. They're easy to describe and understand. This clarity extends to their pricing models, which are usually transparent and simple, aiding clients when comparing offerings and making informed decisions.

It's crucial that your material offering directly addresses the material needs of your clients. While it's also beneficial to connect with their immaterial needs (the emotional, the brand-related), this often introduces intangible elements into the offering. Balancing the tangible with the intangible is key, ensuring your offering resonates on all levels.

One significant benefit of having a clear, tangible offering is the ability to diversify and optimize sales channels. Tangible products and services can be effectively marketed through a variety of platforms, encompassing traditional retail, e-commerce, direct sales, and distribution partners.

1. **List your physical or packaged offering.**

2. Link it to the physical need it serves.

3. Link to the intangible needs it serves.

4. Also link to the intangible elements that accompany or boost the effect of the material offering.

5. Identify discontinuities and illogicalities.

   There are some examples on the next spread.

DEVELOPMENT TIME

At this point, you may want to revisit and amend your client needs. You can do that, of course, but I recommend that you complete the whole map before doing so.

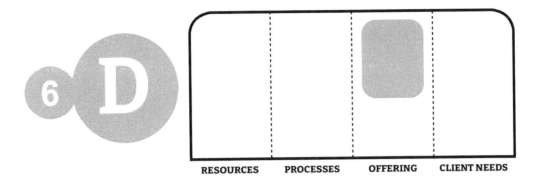

RESOURCES   **PROCESSES**   **OFFERING**   **CLIENT NEEDS**

IMMATERIAL OFFERING

This part of your offering is often overlooked yet crucially significant. It is tied to your client's non-material needs, covering the emotional, cognitive, and relational.

These elements are characterized by their elasticity. Unlike physical products that maintain a static form, immaterial offerings are highly personalized and adaptive.

The most difficult challenge in this immaterial landscape is working out how to articulate and commercialize these offerings. Their fluidity and vagueness, while being sources of adaptability and personalization, also make them hard to define in conventional terms.

Digital elements like apps, software, and data streams may also find their place in this upper part of the fold. They are frequently packaged and presented in ways that lend them a more tangible feel. This dual nature allows them to occasionally migrate lower down the map, especially when they are commercialized or materialized in more concrete forms.

1. **List things that create personalized and reciprocal connections with clients.**

2. How do you help them grow and improve?

3. How do you help them fulfill their purpose?

4. List brand elements relevant to the client.

5. List places of interaction like discussion forums or communities.

6. List fully tailored, human-powered services.

7. How are they linked to your client's needs?

8. What is the intimacy level between you and your clients?

9. Is there constant dialogue?

Examples LET'S SIMPLIFY THINGS: PRODUCTS DOWN, SERVICES UP.

Food delivery services like Doordash or Uber Eats are able to tempt users by offering an anywhere, all-the-time interface via an app that allows for abundance in food. They remove the need for a consumer to venture to a restaurant or supermarket. This offering is coupled with a reliable and predictable delivery service, as well as a simple pricing model. But the bedrock of the service is the food.

App: Selection

Delivery

Restaurants

App: Pricing

Food

RESOURCES   PROCESSES   **OFFERING**   CLIENT NEEDS

Consultancy

Product 1

Product 2

Product 3

A consultancy company can package its services to resemble products. This means it needs to have a fixed process, outcomes, and pricing. But it does not mean that the company should end its customized consulting.
Products can help clients better understand the consultancy's offering. They also provide evidence of the company's ability to identify tangible outcomes for its clients even when they procure customized services.

PROCESSES   **OFFERING**   CLIENT NEEDS

COMMUNITY PYRAMID

Developed by Ghost Community, this process tool helps develop all kinds of business communities.

Following these six steps will help you pace your journey and understand what the community needs next.

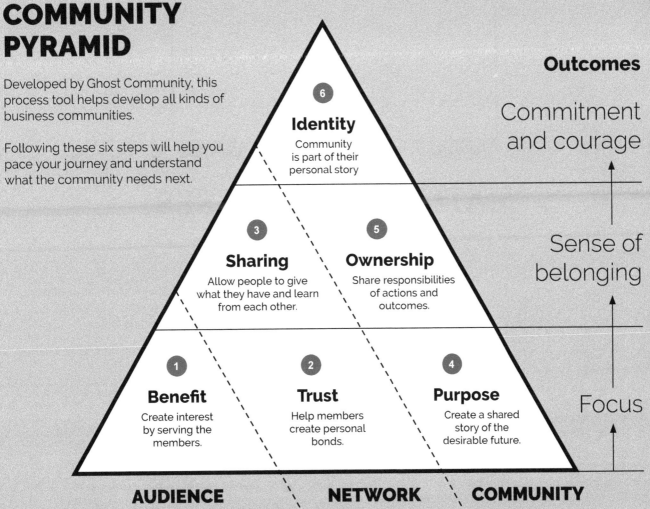

Outcomes

Commitment and courage

Sense of belonging

Focus

6 Identity
Community is part of their personal story

3 Sharing
Allow people to give what they have and learn from each other.

5 Ownership
Share responsibilities of actions and outcomes.

1 Benefit
Create interest by serving the members.

2 Trust
Help members create personal bonds.

4 Purpose
Create a shared story of the desirable future.

AUDIENCE   **NETWORK**   **COMMUNITY**

Building internal, client, and partner communities helps companies stay relevant, exchange knowledge, and better understand needs. Communities can predict industry trends and help carve a shared path for the future.
Community is a great way to increase the flow of intangible elements and allow a company to be an integral part of that flow.

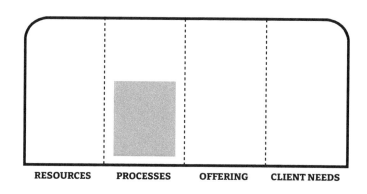

RESOURCES   **PROCESSES**   **OFFERING**   **CLIENT NEEDS**

MATERIAL PROCESSES

How do we do it?

Tangible processes refer to the physical, observable actions that create a product or deliver a service. A variety of elements are blended to produce the final offering.

These processes are crucial because they involve the direct manipulation of physical resources, which are often the backbone of product-based businesses.

Developing the processes can be slow and expensive, requires significant investment of capital, expertise, and time. It is strategically imperative, therefore, that businesses determine which processes they should own and which can be outsourced.

Owning certain key processes can create a substantial competitive advantage. The processes that a company chooses to develop and maintain in-house can become unique selling points.

1. **List physical actions required to produce your offering.** Don't worry if you mix resources and processes to start with. You can always sort them out later on.

2. Put the slow, expensive, and time-consuming processes at the bottom.

3. Move the "lighter" processes to the middle of the fold.

DEVELOPMENT TIME

Consider these questions:

How can you make the processes lighter?
Can you simplify, streamline, or make them more efficient? Can you stop doing them?

What data can you extract?
What data is easily available and what would yield valuable insights?

What parts of the process do you want to protect?
Can you identify the critical elements that will create your competitive advantage?

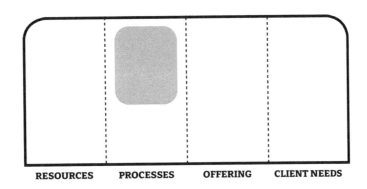

RESOURCES   **PROCESSES**   **OFFERING**   **CLIENT NEEDS**

IMMATERIAL PROCESSES

This is the area of the map where everything should flow. Everything!

At the heart of your company's ecosystem lies a dynamic, flowing network of immaterial processes. This is a realm where knowledge, skills, talent, and understanding aren't just stored, but move and evolve. The success of your company depends on how effectively you facilitate and accelerate these flows. Think of these processes as the lifeblood of your organization. They keep it alive, enable it to thrive, and connect it to the outer world.

As these processes are often intangible, they are difficult to measure. In fact, they remain hard to recognize until their absence is felt.

The integration of AI into these immaterial processes is indispensable. AI can dramatically enhance the flow of information and knowledge within a company.

A company that effectively integrates AI into its immaterial processes will not only streamline operations but also foster a culture of continuous innovation and learning. However, the adoption of AI must be approached strategically. It involves not only the technical integration of AI tools but also a cultural shift within the organization.

It's crucial to maintain an open mind, encouraging external elements to permeate your organizational boundaries, fostering reciprocal relationships with the surrounding world. A company that excels in managing these immaterial processes is not only prepared for the future but is actively shaping it with current knowledge and cutting-edge innovation that are constantly refreshed.

1. **List processes that connect intangible resources to your offering.**

2. List cooperation processes.

3. List processes that boost learning and innovation.

4. List valuable data streams.

5. List automated digital processes.

6. List key algorithms and AI applications.

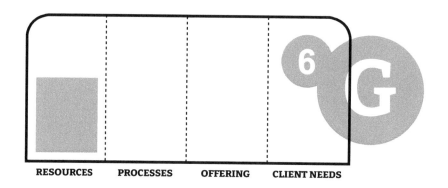

RESOURCES   PROCESSES   OFFERING   CLIENT NEEDS

MATERIAL RESOURCES

In the tangible realm of your company lie the material resources, the concrete elements that you can touch, see, and feel. They are like Lego bricks, each holding the potential to build something greater.

The value of these resources is amplified when they are unique and safeguarded from competitors. If they mirror what your competitors possess, they may become burdens rather than assets.

A critical aspect of managing these material resources is recognizing that many of your resources are combinations of both material and immaterial elements. For example, a piece of technology is not just a physical device but also encompasses the intellectual property, design, and innovation that went into its creation.

It is crucial to unbundle these elements, to identify both the physical resource and its intangible value. This unbundling allows for a deeper understanding of each resource's true potential and worth.

1. **List your physical resources.**

2. List elements that behave like tangible resources, such as patents.

3. Unbundle the immaterial from the material (e.g., The expert and their expertise).

4. List assets that are owned by someone else but used by you.

DEVELOPMENT TIME

1. How do you protect your unique material assets?

2. How do you replace unnecessary tangible resources with something lighter?

3. Do you need to own things?

4. What resources can you get from your ecosystem?

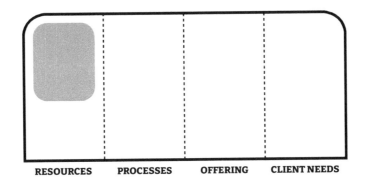

RESOURCES   PROCESSES   OFFERING   CLIENT NEEDS

IMMATERIAL RESOURCES

Immaterial resources are often the hidden gems that propel companies to greatness. Let's start with knowledge, the most important immaterial resource you have, no matter the size of your company. Others include experience, vision, social connections, courage, empathy, and data. These are often the driving forces behind innovation and growth.

Traditional business models may not look beyond the company's walls when considering these resources. This is a mistake. A forward-thinking approach recognizes that the entire world can be an immense reservoir of immaterial resources, if we are willing to open our doors and guide these resources in.

The reciprocal exchange of information is essential. It's not merely about acquiring knowledge from the world, it's also about sharing your own insights and resources. This exchange fosters a symbiotic relationship where all parties benefit and grow. It creates an ecosystem of shared learning and development, where the cumulative knowledge is greater than the sum of its parts.

Incorporating this approach of openness into your business model transforms how immaterial resources are viewed and utilized. It shifts the focus from internal resource management to a dynamic, global network of knowledge and innovation.

1. **List your internal immaterial resources.**

2. List the external resources to which you have access.

DEVELOPMENT TIME

1. Identify which external immaterial resources, if accessed, could significantly benefit your business.

2. How do you ensure that you retain the resources you have now in the future?

3. Evaluate if certain immaterial resources or processes are so critical that they require protection. Consider legal protections like patents, as well as integration into your company's narrative, so that they become synonymous with your brand.

How to build your strategy

It all starts with understanding your clients' needs.
Personally, I would love to start from with resources and
processes, but I have to accept that clients are
somehow more important for business.
Without them, there is no business.

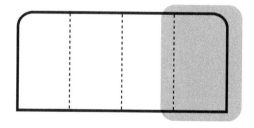

SEE ALL POSSIBLE NEEDS

Understanding client needs is crucial, particularly in balancing the tangible and intangible. Clients often seek something tangible, or at least something they perceive as tangible. This tangibility acts as a token of exchange, a concrete symbol of value in a business transaction. Yet, the true value of a product or service often transcends its physical form.

In B2B procurement processes, the need for tangibility is evident—for example, when forming complex engineering partnerships or crafting extensive training programs. Clients want to integrate these services into their existing processes, to see and measure their "real" impact. They demand strict deadlines and KPIs, not just as metrics of success, but as a way to ground their investments in the physical world. This approach, treating services as tangible assets, reveals a deeper quest for certainty and measurable outcomes in business dealings.

Despite our self-perception as rational buyers, emotions significantly influence our decisions. This interplay material outcomes and emotions is key in understanding client behavior. Intangible needs often outweigh tangible results. These needs can be cognitive, like learning something new, or emotional and social, such as the desire for belonging, recognition, or a heightened self-image.

Consider, for example, the act of purchasing a cup of coffee from a well-known brand like _____. The tangible product—the coffee—represents only a fraction of the value. The intangible benefits—the experience, connection to the brand, and sense of exclusivity—play a significant role in the customer's choice.

Understanding client needs requires that we recognize the entire spectrum from the tangible to the intangible. The tangible elements are easier to quantify and measure.

A comprehensive strategy must account for both tangible and intangible client needs. Understanding this interplay allows for more effective and empathetic business strategies, ensuring that offerings not only meet the immediate, tangible requirements but also resonate on a deeper, more emotional level. There is often a fear when catering to deeper, unspoken client needs and incorporating these into a company's strategy. This involves recognizing the emotional factors in decision-making and providing value that resonates at a deeper level.

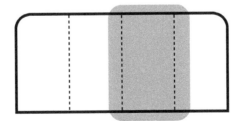

BALANCE YOUR OFFERING

In strategizing your business offering, understanding the spectrum from the material to the immaterial is crucial. This spectrum ranges from concrete, stable, and manageable products to more fluid, responsive services, often termed solutions. Understanding this helps us aligning our offerings with the diverse needs of our clients.

Let's look at men's suits to illustrate this idea:

Bespoke Suits: At the immaterial end of the spectrum, bespoke suits represent a service-oriented approach. Here, the tailor engages in a dialogue with the client, tailoring not just the suit but the entire process to meet both practical and emotional needs. This is a classic example of a service that adapts and responds to individual client requirements.

Made-to-Measure Suits: Sitting in the middle, made-to-measure suits offer a blend of product and service. Clients select from pre-existing templates, which are then adjusted to better fit their measurements. This option offers a compromise between personalization and the convenience of pre-made designs.

Ready-to-Wear (Off-the-Rack): At the product end, off-the-rack suits are about materiality—standard sizes, immediate availability, and tangible attributes. These suits cater to clients looking for quick-to-access and straightforward solutions without the need for personalization.

Focusing on products means prioritizing material qualities—ease of understanding, straightforward ownership, and simple pricing. Products allow clients to make clear comparisons based on tangible attributes. They are typically less adaptable but offer consistency and reliability.

Services, on the other hand, are designed to meet the intangible needs of clients. They are more adaptable, require lower upfront investments, and can evolve quickly to respond to changing client needs. Services often focus on building deeper connections with clients, addressing their evolving expectations in a personalized manner.

In reality, the distinction between products and services is often blurred. Many product-based companies offer sales services, while service-oriented firms package their offerings to resemble products for easier understanding and purchase.

Fully digital products and services represent a unique blend of both. They combine the control and ease of understanding typical of material products

Use case

Competitor analysis

Map competitor business models. Seek out the differences from your own.

YOUR MAP

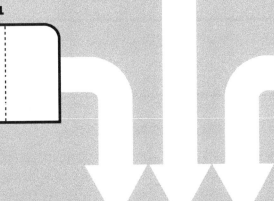

COMPETITOR 1

COMPETITOR 2

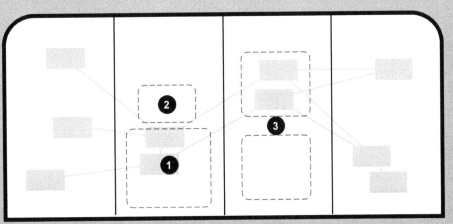

1 There will be many overlaps between your own strategy and the rest of the industry.

2 Look for the gaps.

3 Difference is an opportunity.

with the scalability, cost-effectiveness, and rapid evolution characteristic of immaterial services. Digital offerings are particularly adept at gathering and utilizing data to enhance their value proposition.

Determining the right mix of material and immaterial offerings depends on understanding our clients' needs. Are we addressing their tangible needs with products or their intangible needs with services? Are we combining both? The key lies in recognizing the diverse needs of our clientele and adapting our offerings to meet these needs effectively.

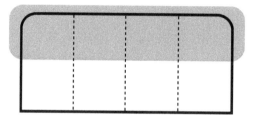

CREATE FLOWS

In the contemporary business landscape, the concept of flow is pivotal, particularly within the intangible realm. Flow represents the dynamic, ever-evolving streams of data, knowledge, and resources that characterize today's digital and interconnected world.

Increasingly, businesses are recognizing the importance of flows in ecosystems, marketplaces, and communities. By adopting a stream lens, companies can identify and engage with these flows, transforming their approach to resources and relationships.

Clients are not just consumers but participants in these flows. Their interactions, data, and feedback are valuable to these streams, helping to foster closer relationships and enriching the company-client dynamic.

Integrating these flows into business operations enhances resilience. By remaining up to date with external streams of information, an agile company can respond to changes in the market and consumer behavior.

Ecosystem mapping

EXTRA

Understanding the strategies and needs of potential members is a crucial step before building a business ecosystem. By identifying what these members lack, you can create a compelling value proposition for them to join the ecosystem. This is a force that can be used also for evil, for example, in the case of Amazon where ecosystem is lead too strongly by one anchor party.

Some examples of strategic gaps that make a great invitation for ecosystem

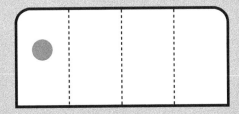 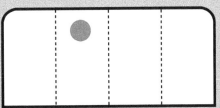 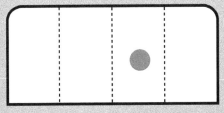

RESOURCES

Data is a valuable asset for businesses looking to enhance decision-making, understand market trends, and personalize customer experiences.

An ecosystem can facilitate data sharing and pooling, allowing members to gain insights they couldn't achieve independently.

PROCESSES

Innovation can be resource-intensive and risky.

Shared innovation processes in an ecosystem can distribute these risks and resources, making it easier for members to experiment and innovate. You can offer partnerships with innovative startups and academic institutions.

OFFERING

Expanding market reach and scaling sales operations is often a challenge for businesses.

By being part of an ecosystem, members can access new channels and markets through other members, scaling more quickly and efficiently.

For flows to be effectively integrated into a business, a significant shift in management perspective is often required. This includes opening up company processes to external flows and participating reciprocally in these streams. It's about embracing openness and exchange.

Companies should focus on creating and nurturing various types of flows:

Data Flows: Harnessing and sharing data streams to enhance decision-making and innovation.

Learning Flows: Continuous learning and knowledge sharing within and outside the organization.

Talent Flows: Encouraging the movement and development of talent within different areas of the company and beyond.

Business Flows: Streamlining business processes to be more adaptive and interconnected with external environments.

Adopting a flow approach necessitates a change in organizational mindset. Internal processes should be viewed as opportunities to integrate external elements and share these flows to strengthen them. It's about moving from a static to a dynamic, interconnected way of operating.

Management's role in fostering business flows is transformative, involving not just a strategic shift but also a cultural and operational overhaul.

At the forefront of this transformation is the need for management to adopt a stream lens. This perspective views the organization not as a standalone entity but as part of a dynamic ecosystem of interconnected flows. Leading this shift from traditional, siloed operations to a network-oriented approach is foundational. In doing so, leadership is responsible for cultivating an organizational culture that values the sharing and exchange of information. This openness must extend beyond the internal mechanisms of the company to include clients, partners, and the broader market. Such a culture is essential for tapping into and contributing to the wider flows of knowledge and resources.

Another critical aspect is redefining what constitutes a resource. Management must guide the organization in recognizing that intangible assets, such as client data, employee expertise, and market insights, are just as crucial as physical assets. These intangible elements form the backbone of business flows. Client interactions, for instance, are not merely transactions but valuable resources. By viewing these interactions as integral to the flow of resources, management can convert them into actionable insights and opportunities for innovation.

Integrating external flows of information into the company's internal processes is another strategic move to maintain agility and responsiveness. Management's oversight in this integration ensures that the organization remains adaptable to market changes. However, this must be balanced with potential risks, fostering an environment that is both flexible and resilient.

A key responsibility of management in supporting flows is ensuring active participation in the give-and-take of resources. This reciprocity not only enhances the company's value in its network and ecosystems but also mandates strategic decisions on what and how much to share without compromising competitive advantages.

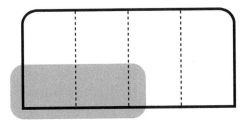

OWN ONLY THE IMPORTANT THINGS

The concept of ownership in a business context is nuanced and multifaceted. It's about finding the perfect balance between safeguarding what's essential for your company's identity and success, and staying open to collaboration, innovation, and the flow of ideas.

At the heart of ownership lies control—over resources, ideas, and direction. This control, while necessary, can often lead to a reduction in movement, flow, and the opportunity for serendipity—those happy, unforeseen accidents that sometimes lead to significant breakthroughs.

The concept of poisonous ownership is particularly pertinent for businesses. When a company clings too tightly to what it owns, it risks stifling creativity and innovation. For a small company, this could mean an inward focus, playing a small game that limits its potential. For larger companies, the impact of excessive ownership manifests in different ways: unidirectional partnerships, internal silos, and a reluctance to venture beyond the familiar.

A company bogged down by too much ownership often is unable to discern what's crucial for its growth and what's merely excess baggage. This lack of clarity can prevent the company from setting a definitive direction and moving forward. Similarly, a company with low self-esteem might hoard its resources and ideas, shying away from engaging with other businesses, sharing unfinished ideas, or discussing strategies openly.

EXAMPLE: PATENTS

Patents illustrate the balance between control and the flow of ideas. Originally conceived to protect inventors, they grant the exclusive right to produce and use an invention. However, this control comes with a unique twist: the patent application process necessitates the public disclosure of the invention's details. This requirement serves a dual purpose. It protects the inventor's rights while simultaneously sowing the seeds for future innovation, as others can build upon the publicly available knowledge.

An extreme example of this is a company so burdened by its possessions that it becomes like Smaug, the dragon from Tolkien's Middle-earth, curled protectively over its treasures. This image serves as a metaphor for companies so obsessed with guarding what they own that they become immobilized, unable to innovate or respond to market changes.

Despite these pitfalls, it is crucial to acknowledge that ownership is vital for a company's identity and success. The key is to own the right things—those that define and distinguish your company. This could include unique resources, talented individuals, or innovative processes.

Ownership needs to be strategic and intentional. It's not just about safeguarding your assets from competitors, though that is certainly one aspect. It involves integrating these assets into the very fabric of your company—its processes, culture, and brand identity. This integration makes replication by others significantly more difficult and cements your unique place in the market.

In the age of growing immaterial influence, it is vital for companies to understand how loosening their ownership can help them access intangible flows.

Questions to think about

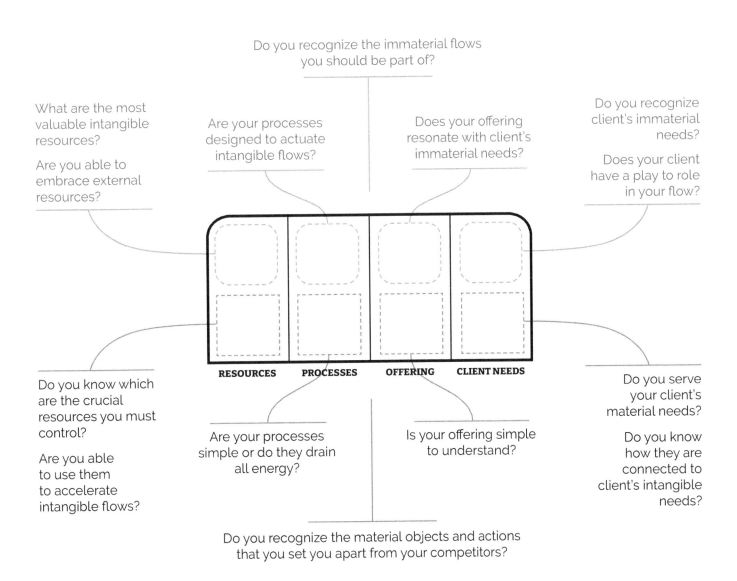

Do you recognize the immaterial flows you should be part of?

What are the most valuable intangible resources?

Are you able to embrace external resources?

Are your processes designed to actuate intangible flows?

Does your offering resonate with client's immaterial needs?

Do you recognize client's immaterial needs?

Does your client have a play to role in your flow?

RESOURCES **PROCESSES** **OFFERING** **CLIENT NEEDS**

Do you know which are the crucial resources you must control?

Are you able to use them to accelerate intangible flows?

Are your processes simple or do they drain all energy?

Is your offering simple to understand?

Do you serve your client's material needs?

Do you know how they are connected to client's intangible needs?

Do you recognize the material objects and actions that you set you apart from your competitors?

Last words

The reign of the immaterial is not a distant prophecy; it is the vibrant ecosystem of our present existence. Humanity has always excelled in conjuring wonders from the ether of thought, turning intangible dreams into tangible realities. With each technological leap, the doors to this immaterial world swing wider, ushering in an era of exponential growth and unimaginable possibilities.

This shift, most evident in technology and business, poses an extraordinary challenge to leaders both today and in the future. It demands new perspectives and a willingness to unlearn the old. Our practices and thought patterns, so deeply entrenched in the tangible, must now adapt to a paradigm where the physical is just one aspect of reality. We are asked to envision a world not of static objects, but of dynamic, perpetual flows, where our role is not to control but to enhance and amplify.

The stark contrast between the old and the new is most palpable in corporations, entities born to expedite physical processes. Here, companies find themselves at a crossroads, navigating between the allure of the new immaterial value and the weight of traditional expectations. Move too swiftly, and you risk Icarus's fate; lag too far behind, and obsolescence beckons.

For every leader navigating these turbulent times, the challenge is as daunting as it is exhilarating. As we forge ahead, it is crucial to recognize the strategic opportunities presented by the intangible realm. This is not about abandoning the tangible but about harmoniously blending its solidity and reliability with the fluidity and boundless potential of the intangible. By interweaving these realms, businesses can sculpt strategies that are not only resilient but also primed for a future that is as unpredictable as it is promising. Let us embrace this new era with open minds and hearts, ready to explore the infinite possibilities that lie in the convergence of the material and immaterial worlds.

●
I'm done.
This nonsense
has completely
drained me. As
Churchill signed off,
"I'm bored with it all."

Printed in the USA
CPSIA information can be obtained
at www.ICGtesting.com
LVHW071138021224
798108LV00012B/238